Birthmarks

True Stories from Real Mothers

Edited By Brooke Nelson

ISBN: 978-0-578-77912-6 (paperback)

Book design by Sam Berkes

To my mom, for being my first teacher, my biggest fan, and also for looking away when I pooped on the table. Twice.

And should she choose to be a Mother one day, be my eyes, Lord, that I may see her, lying on a blanket on the floor at 4:50am, all-at-once exhausted, bored, and in love with the little creature whose poop is leaking up its back. "My mother did this for me once," she will realize as she cleans feces off her baby's neck. "My mother did this for me."

—*Tina Fey*, Bossypants

Contents

Introduction

By Brooke Nelson

Mothers touch the beginning of something. The Thing. We grow the People. We hang out for nine months and then we meet each other naked, body to body, fluid to fluid. Our children, our microchimerisms, leave their DNA behind in our bodies. Microscopic mementos. These children physically become part of us for life; their cells swirl in us, infiltrate, literally become our beating hearts. And then we have to allow them to be them. They are not our reproductions; they are their own productions. We are simply the coordinators of life: theirs and ours and we have to make it cohesive. We have to find our freedom to allow their freedom. And it's hard. It's hard to be someone's Everyone and also our own Everyone and still have the ability to not only see where autonomy is necessary but then be able to facilitate it. At the distress of us, the mothers. We assess all of the mistakes of our own parents and try to fix it in ourselves. We won't or we will regarding our pasts. We care too much or not enough and we never know if what we choose is right. And having that responsibility and power is gratifying and terrifying and eternal.

The narratives in this collection vary as much as those who wrote them, and they demonstrate the weight of the responsibility and power of motherhood. I asked these women to contribute their stories of conception, pregnancy, birth, postpartum, and parenting as a means of sharing honestly in a time when such honesty is fleeting. Technology and evolving social constructs have isolated us from the community so necessary in mothering; we are an out-loud secret society and we need not be. We should not be. Mothering is hard, and attempts at connecting to other mothers in an honest way is often masked by a facade of very curated social media posts. The smiling kids at the park. The delicious homemade family dinner. The clean house in the background. This collection aims to shine the light on some realities of motherhood: the mom on her phone while her kids play at the park, the dishes piled in the sink from the family dinner, the loads of laundry shoved in the corner, just out of view of the camera.

We are only our stories, and sharing these with others will bind us to the sisterhood of mothering, connect us to the children we want or don't want or have or lost, and keep truthful the realities of raising people.

Introduction

The women who contributed to this collective were diverse in their experiences, if not in other ways. I was limited in my pool in the same ways we are limited in anything: through our education levels, our careers, our ages, our socioeconomic status, our race, and in geography. While I wish I could have gathered contributions and therefore experiences greater than in my immediate reach, the voices within are still valuable.

The expressions from these mothers demonstrate the bodily and emotional aspects associated with motherhood, but more importantly, they prove that we are all a little scarred. Our children scar us from the beginning. They stretch our bodies. They move our bones. They alter our literal hearts just a bit, changing us in painfully good ways; these stories shine light on the lasting mark mothering makes on us. These scars are inevitable, but heal tougher than flesh, and these stories aim to demonstrate such strength.

Things About Birthing a Human and Becoming a New Mom That You Should Know

By Erica Fleming

1. The shit that comes out of you after you birth someone can be horrific. I'm talking straight-up, crime-scene toilet. Clots the size of a baseball. For WEEKS. Yup. Fun fact: even if you have a C-section, you still get this experience. Yay!

2. The hideous hospital underwear are very necessary. Hoard ALL OF THE MESH UNDERWEAR. Yes, they are ugly as hell. Get over yourself. Take them before you leave.

3. Did you know that even if your legs don't swell during pregnancy, they can still swell after? Cankle City. Population: You.

4. You will probably feel some murdery feelings toward your husband or partner. Multiply that by five if you are breast-feeding.

5. Speaking of breastfeeding, for something so natural, it's actually hard as fuck. So. many. things. can go wrong. And you will probably blame yourself for all of them. You will leak, your tits will get hard as rocks, and your

nipples will crack and bleed. Or you won't have enough milk and you will feel like a failure. You will cry. But, it will get better. Maybe.

6. Your husband may take to parenthood like a duck to water, or like a whale to the sky. If the latter is the case, you may have to tell him exactly what to do for a while. Try not to snark while doing it, though. Okay, sometimes is fine.

7. The hormones. Oh, the hormones. You will cry about everything and the sad will hit you like a freight train. Even if you weren't emotional during pregnancy, this can still be a thing. Eventually, you should even back out and emotions should turn (slowly) back to normal.

8. HOWEVER. If the hormones keep up and/or lead you to scarier shit, you might have to seek medical help. Postpartum depression is more common than you think and can sneak up on you well after you have the baby.

9. You will probably smell. Like, really bad. Old milk, sweat, spit up, and even maple syrup (thanks, fenugreek!) can all add to your brand new mom-stank.

10. Sleep will become an elusive unicorn that remains juuuust out of reach for the next five years, minimum. Childless acquaintances will complain of being "soooo tired!" from the six hours they clocked the night before. You will want to punch them. Repeatedly.

11. You will mourn your prepartum body and chastise Old You for ever believing that you were fat. You will also curse your postpartum body for looking the way it does, while simultaneously marveling at what you were able to create, sustain, and birth in nine months. Hopefully, however, you will eventually realize that you were beautiful before and you are beautiful now. Period.

12. Meaningful adult interaction is seldom, so you'll find yourself doing anything at all to connect with someone who can speak and understand English. Partner gets home from work: hope you've got your listening ears on, pal.

13. You might not feel the "rush of love" that new moms talk about. Maybe not right away, or maybe not for a while. Either way, you aren't broken or defective. It's hormones, mama.

14. Every parenting decision you will make, from whether to breastfeed or bottle feed, to picking the best brand of diaper cream, will be agonized over.

15. You might not want visitors. Want to hole up in your house and not communicate with the outside world for a minimum of two weeks? You do you, girl.

16. You also might crave visitors so they can tend to the baby while you tend to yourself. Nap? Shower? Hot meal? Hand that baby off and you can have it all!

17. You might want to return to work and you might not. Regardless, be sure that you have a support system in place. You might be the most independent person in the history of ever, but that all can change once you have to leave your baby. Reach out to other friends at work who can boost you up, clear your schedule after work so you can focus on your baby, and soak up all the moments you can. And check in often with your partner, especially if you've been dealing with postpartum depression.

18. Having kids is really fucking hard. They engage every molecule of your body, every spot in your brain, every second of your existence. Your world revolves around cluster feedings and sleep schedules and meticulously planning your day just so you can walk around Target for thirty minutes. You might cry because your tits hurt, because you just love your baby so much, because you miss your old self, or for NO FUCKING REASON AT ALL. It sucks, and it's okay to admit that it sucks.

19. But mama, it will get better. You might wistfully think back on all the extra time you had that you no longer have, the spontaneity you used to enjoy, and all the date nights you once had with your partner. But then, your baby starts to recognize you. They smile at you. Laugh for you. Clap for you. Reach for you. Walk to you. You find that little by little, it isn't such a chore to leave the house, and you are able to figure out a schedule that isn't ALL about the baby. And that love that you might not feel just yet? It will come. At some point, it will come. And when it does, every damn thing makes sense.

20. Lastly, everyone who has had a kid (and those who haven't) will give you parenting advice. Don't take any of it if you don't want to, including advice on this list. Ultimately, you

know your baby the best, and the decisions you are making right now won't scar them for life. You are the boss. So, that unsolicited advice? Don't feel bad about not taking it.

DeKalb, IL, 1974

By Susan Eby

Taken from my journal just after my first child, Aaron's, birth. Comments in brackets added for clarification.

My water broke at Dad's house while I was talking to Jim, my husband at the time, on the phone. [He was downtown, I think at a bar, ostensibly working on a project.] I asked Jim to come get me and I ran to the bathroom. It was the weirdest feeling—the time had actually come—I didn't know what would happen next. Dad yelled up the stairs at Lori and Shari [my sisters, ages fourteen and eleven], and said I was going to the hospital. Everybody was very excited. I think dad was concerned that I might be hemorrhaging, as that's what happened to mom when she had me. I was her firstborn, and I was about to deliver my firstborn. Jim arrived and I had to wear my wet clothes to the hospital since I didn't bring a change, and being December, it was cold. I shook all the way there, though part of it was nervousness, too. When I got to the room at the hospital, we discovered I had already dilated to eight centimeters! I was in transition! [Jim had not participated in Lamaze classes, and I don't think he was interested in being in the delivery room. In hindsight, I now know that he was seeing someone else at that time, and though we didn't know it at the time, I think he may have been having a manic episode of bipolar disorder, so he probably was a bit conflicted.] It seemed like forever until my doctor arrived. In the meantime, with my sister-in-law, Jacki [conveniently, a nurse at that hospital and on duty at the time] coaching, I pushed my heart out and Aaron was really ready to be born.

Before my doctor assisted in the delivery, he had the nerve to smoke a cigarette in the delivery room doorway. [It was 1974.] I remember thinking, "Put out that blasted cigarette and get in here!" What an unclean atmosphere. A couple times I lost my composure while trying to do Lamaze breathing, but Jacki got me back on track. Then, finally after one big push, Aaron came all the way out of me. I cried for joy and so did one of the nurses. It was the most fantastic feeling I had ever had. I felt so excited and exhilarated, and it really was indescribable. All of this happened in just one hour and fifteen minutes. I remember one of the nurses commenting that these women who use Lamaze techniques seem to deliver really quickly, and this was no exception.

My hospital roommate and I were up half the night, sharing our experiences. We had the best time. We were feeling so much awe—both of us. It was truly the most fantastic experience of my life.

First Pregnancy, 1980

By Sylvia Norton

My first indication of pregnancy was puking in the parking lot at work. I refused to believe it was anything other than the stomach flu. I had only been married a few months, and I was nineteen years old. This, however, was no flu.

As my pregnancy continued, I pretty much did everything as if I wasn't pregnant: bowling, four-wheeling, swimming, dancing, etc. Aside from morning sickness and exhaustion, I felt good and strong and the same as before I was pregnant. However, as my belly got bigger, so too did my butt. This had me worried. I was terrified I would be huge forever after this baby. That was my only fear.

Baby was due December 10th. December 10th came and went. The only thing more grumpy than a nine-months-pregnant woman is a nine-months-pregnant woman who is past her due date. My then-husband, Stan, and I did everything possible to coax this baby out.

Spicy food, walking, sex. In desperation, we took the 4x4 off-road and hit as many big bumps as we could find. Still nothing. I began to give up hope and believe this baby would live inside me forever. Then, eight days later, my girl decided to make her entrance.

Her father was getting a root canal and I didn't want him to miss his appointment. I was convinced I was not going into labor any time soon, so I saw no issue with this. I told him it would probably take a long time even if I did go into labor, so I encouraged him to go ahead and get the root canal. Business as usual. My best friend came over and stayed with me while he had his procedure. I had been having some contractions off and on and she asked me how far apart they were. I had no clue. Suspecting that I was further along than I believed, she decided to time them. They were three to four minutes apart. We were having a baby.

My best friend freaked out and called the dentist's office looking for my husband. They said he had already left so we thought he'd be home soon. We waited and waited. But no Stan. My friend was getting ready to take me to the hospital, as my contractions were intensifying, when he finally got home. She yelled at him, "Where were you?" and he said he was getting his truck washed. In December. On a cold day. I think he and I were both in denial as to what was going to happen on this winter day.

When I got to the hospital, I only had a little time before my daughter arrived. I pushed a few times, dry-heaved, and then she was born. I was immediately in love. Big love.

This little girl was perfect, but my body was not. Amid snuggling and loving my new baby, I was so determined to get my body back that I did five sit-ups the day I delivered. Then I did ten the next day, and fifteen the day after that. I continued this for months. I immediately started dieting and I could not lose that weight. It took me six months before I lost the last pesky ten pounds.

It was hard having a baby in the dead of winter. The holidays and family parties were over. It was January, cold, cloudy, and dark. I sat in my daughter's room in a borrowed rocking chair and felt a heavy sadness. I would look at my sweet, healthy, beautiful baby and feel so guilty for being so sad. This lasted only two weeks, but it was a horrific feeling. A sinking, foggy, claustrophobic sadness that I will never forget.

After those two weeks, I regained some of myself and really started enjoying my life as a mother. My daughter was my living doll. I dressed her everyday in dresses and tights, all hand-medowns from my sister, all totally adorable. We had no money, but I had big plans for my baby. My daughter was strong-willed and difficult, but I loved being her mother and I couldn't wait to be her mom everyday for the rest of my life.

Reflections on a Year of Becoming a Mother

By Lori Berkes-Nelson

Introduction

When I was sixteen, my mother threatened me with, "You're going to have a daughter just like you someday!" It wasn't said because I was the perfect daughter. I was strong-willed, outspoken, opinionated, and rebelling against change. I replied, "That's just fine because I will treat her the way a daughter should be treated!"

My father died when I was fifteen, and my mom coped by drinking. She soon remarried an abusive alcoholic and my needs were not a priority. Out of necessity, I became a self-sufficient young adult and developed a protective emotional shell. How would I ever become a good mother? How could I ever love unconditionally when my own mother chose alcohol and an alcoholic over a grieving daughter during a crucial period of development? How would I know how a daughter should be treated?

When the ultrasound said she was a girl, I was not surprised. I was going to have a daughter just like me. It was inevitable. I was terrified I would screw this up.

May 8, 1997

I became a mother today! When they placed that beautiful little girl on my chest and I began to talk to her and welcome her to life outside of me, she stopped crying and looked deep into me. I thought I would be sad that she was no longer a part of my body, but it was far from the truth. She felt more a part of me than anything I had ever felt.

August 10, 1997

It's the night before I have to return to work after being with you every day. I held you and rocked you before I laid you down, and I couldn't stop crying. I even prayed to win the lottery so that I wouldn't have to work. If you had told me a year ago that I would feel like this, I would not have believed it. I've loved my career—it's such a large part of who I am. I just didn't know how much I would love being a mom. Your mom.

September 19, 1997

Last night, Daddy was at a friend's house. You and I slept on the couch, you on my chest, our hearts beating together as they did for nine months. I couldn't put you down. I know that you are changing every day, and I don't want to miss a second of it.

October 21, 1997

People ask me all the time, "How's your baby?" And, I can only ever say "Great!" Because you are great! Yesterday you sprouted your first tooth. Time marches on.

My career used to be the most important thing in my life before I became a mother. I am still committed to being the best professional, but now I've added mom to my resume and I am committed to being the best mom I can. It's hard to balance the two. I have committed to breastfeeding for an entire year—it requires pumping at work, and thank goodness I have my own office to do so. Leaving work on time is still difficult to do when there are problems I need to address. There are still phone calls at home and pages. I don't like the interruptions and don't like having to divide my attention.

I also don't like the fact that I only have a few hours a day with you, Monday through Friday. I am afraid that you will be closer to your grandma who is with you all day. I love the weekends with you but they are so short. And then, how do I get the other things in life taken care of? Not enough time...

November 27, 1997

Our first Thanksgiving together since the womb. It is clear to me that we are born with a personality. Yours is fabulous. You have a beautiful spirit and a sense of humor. You are independent and yet love people. I am more and more in love with you every day!

November 28, 1997

I didn't realize how hard it was going to be to be a wife after becoming a mother. I know in my head that my marriage relationship must be a priority for us to be a healthy family, but right now that requires work. Being your mom requires commitment but it doesn't feel like work. I don't know if I can continue to be successful at work and be the mom I want to be. Not sure how to figure all this out. I know it's not in my nature to be a stay-at-home mom, but could I find a happy medium? I'm tired most of the time. I feel like I burn the candle at both ends to try to accomplish the same things as before you were born. I am learning to let some things go. Maybe the floors are dirty or the laundry has piled up. I try not to let it define me.

December 25, 1997

Our first Christmas together as a family. We begin our own

traditions and follow in those that we have been a part of for a long time. You prefer the wrapping paper to anything else.

January 1, 1998

Happy New Year! Top of my gratitude list, my #1 blessing is my beautiful daughter! All the others seem so insignificant. When I look at you, I feel I'm with the ocean. I cannot fully experience my love because it is so enormous that I'm overwhelmed and I get restless.

April 2, 1998

I thought having a baby would slow me down, and instead it has perpetuated my need to do more than one thing at a time. I want to be a good mother, to be attentive to each moment, but at times I am scattered and careless. Today, you fell and hit your head hard on the coffee table and it was my fault because I left you standing there while I went to get the camera. I wanted to take your pain away especially because it was my stupidity that allowed it to happen. I love you so much and still fear all that could happen to take you away from me in an instant. I want to be a good, careful, but not overprotective mother. I want to enjoy all of the moments.

May 8, 1998

Happy Birthday! I have mixed emotions about this milestone. I'm excited for your first birthday, but sad because you really will no longer be a baby. I'm sure I will like this next year, but I loved your first year. I find I am a little less patient with your budding independence. Perhaps it is the controller in me. Perhaps that's part of my fear of this next stage: I am raising you to leave me.

April 29, 2010

I became motherless today. I've been fatherless for thirty-five years, but now I feel orphaned. I never relied on my mom. She relied on me for the past thirty-five years and it was hard. I was not the perfect daughter. I was impatient and critical and selfish and even rude at times. I know I hurt my mom sometimes and yet she always seemed to move on. I didn't. My last words to her were whispered in her ear in that hospital bed, "Please forgive me for anything I've done to hurt you and I forgive you for everything. I love you, Mom."

August 25, 2017

My baby goes to college! Smiling and crying.

Reflection

How is it that twenty-two years have passed and I am still learning to be a mother? Just the other day, my daughter was disappointed that her brother was joining us for a day trip. She said, "I like it when it's just you and me." When I told her that it surprised me because I didn't want to spend time with my mom when I was twenty-two, it hit me deeply that I had altered the cycle somehow. The tears rolled down my face as I realized that I didn't have a daughter just like me. I have **my** daughter and we are okay.

Revolution

By Suzie Berkes

Reflecting back on my mothering experiences over the past thirty-nine years, a full generation ago, I was witness to and participant in an American birthing revolution. This revolution included women taking back their rightful place of control during childbirth, the struggle to go 'back' to breastfeeding as the optimum nutrition and nurturing of infants, the dilemmas and economics of being an at-home parent, as well as the many facets of parenting children in a predominantly white, middle class, American framework.

My birth experience was that of a woman at the tail end of the back-to-nature hippie movement of the sixties and seventies (insert picture here of me with a toddler in a crude baby carrier as I silk-screen T-shirts on the porch for grocery money, while the herb-packaging kit sits on the table waiting to be packaged for *The Neighborhood Co-op* during the toddler's nap time just to get a discount at the natural foods store, and my master's thesis sits in the typewriter next to Noam Chomsky's *Theory of Syntax* resting until after the 4:00am feeding, the 100 jars of home-canned tomatoes, peaches, green beans, and applesauce sit colorfully on the shelves behind me, the bread is rising in the bushel-sized bowl in the oven, and I just found out I am pregnant with my second child, Paul, due a couple weeks after my first master's degree graduation).

The late seventies and early eighties were the coming of age for the baby boom children who were the products of the younger post-World War II or Korean War U.S. veterans like my dad. Increasingly, women were rejecting the birthing practices of the previous two generations of American women as they were becoming more empowered, or "liberated," as was the term at that time. My family dubbed me "Ms. Libby," during high school and my early college years because I was interested in stereotypically male pursuits, such as repairing cars, pumping my own gas, changing car oil, etc.

I'm sure my family's adventure of rejecting the city life for the back-to-the-farm life of southern Illinois had something to do with my awakening to want to live closer to nature. I truly communed with the horses in their stalls after each evening feeding, and I watched the sun setting in the west from my perch in the hayloft many days, reflecting on my strange and new farm experiences like driving tractors, manure spreaders, and three-quarter-ton pickups, and bailing hay, catching renegade piglets, breeding horses, building fences, and cleaning stalls. I loved that fresh world and spent hours contemplating it all.

My view of the world as I moved from my farm home and on to college, marriage and having children, was definitely colored by the progressive upheaval in our culture in terms of the roles of men and women. Scientific and technological progress, governed in the West by mostly white men, ruled the popular practices of birthing and feeding babies in most of the people I knew. Our family members were middle class, they had a year or two of college, and they were primarily small business owners or tradespeople. My mother and her mother were like most women who implicitly trusted and obeyed their male doctors. During birth, they were sedated, and consequently removed from their birth experiences and their babies. I wondered, "were mothers not considered as competent as the male doctors in charge to manage their birth experiences?" This generation of mothers often didn't breastfeed after the birth ordeal because of the traumas and fog of being knocked out by ether, given episiotomies, and having babies removed with forceps. They were groggy, their babies were groggy, and the delay in breastfeeding may have been a factor in the experience I heard from women in my mother's generation about the failure to establish a breastfeeding routine. My mom spoke of this and how ashamed and sad she felt to have had her 'ether' births, forceps deliveries, and drugged-out babies being whisked away to the sterile nursery. I envisioned the babies crying endlessly in sterile hospital isolettes, bottle-fed by nurses, while the women like my mother recuperated from the awful and violating birth trauma for days in the hospital. How awful, and how necessary for my generation not to repeat that unnatural practice.

Knowing my mother's story, and armed with counter-cultural information, I was convinced that birth could be a better, more natural, and perhaps even a spiritual endeavor. Ideally, I thought that this should be done with like-minded people using my internal energy to ride the waves of labor, rejecting labels such as pain and contractions. Energy and focus would bring that baby closer to loving arms. To me, childbirth was bearable if the mindset was focused on the needs of the baby, and I could control a great deal of the process with my good health, good spirit, good community, and appropriate medical intervention if necessary. I had to have an unmedicated baby ready to bond and nurse ASAP, or else who knew what may happen? That was the fear. It was a biased ideology, but I think it was strongly based on the many tales of awful, old-school, Western births of which I wanted no part.

In my fervor to divorce myself from the unnatural birthing process I had observed in my friends and family, I devoured *Spiritual Midwifery,* by Ida May Gaskin, the book that informed many of my ideas about birth practices and my philosophy of nurturing mother, baby, and family. That book and *Immaculate Deception,* by Suzanne Arms, introduced me to a world I previously had no knowledge of since I was a fairly young mother at twenty-two, and I had no "liberal" family members having babies at the time. These authors, these women and mothers and fathers who were forming natural communities and communes across the United States, were taking back their birthing experiences from the problematic hospitals, and they were finding success and happiness (bliss, even) in their non-medicated, non-hospital births. They were even practicing exclusive breastfeeding for the first six months to one year of life. It seemed so open, honest, and natural to me. I was very attracted to the stories, and I even reread these books several times in preparation for each of my babies. My husband, a surgical assistant who was trained as an army medic, was not interested or supportive in any way of a home birth after his medical experiences. I didn't fight his point of view much at the time because I just didn't know what to do and had no community yet of my own to support what seemed logical to me. There were not many people taking back their births around me at that time, and most medical communities had few options until birthing rooms evolved in the 1980s.

My reading into birth and parenting preparation, as well as my connection to the university community of Southern Illinois University in Carbondale the summer before I had my first baby, Sam, led me to some research into birthing and child rearing practices around the world. I read about some of the more "natural" cultures who allowed children to sleep within a family bed system, those that didn't separate their babies into a clinical crib in another room, who breastfed on demand, and those who maintained constant contact with mother or another family caregiver twenty-four seven. It all sounded better to me than what I had observed so far in the United States. This was what I wanted for myself as a soon-to-be mother, and it made sense to me since I rejected most things mainstream in those days.

I wonder, were Jim and I rejecting the status quo of that time and so much of our family and community practices out of generational arrogance, or was this brainwashing and reading into my own biases? Possibly. But more importantly, we were determining what would work for us in our lives as soon-to-be parents. We were not simply following what our parents and the mainstream culture around us had demonstrated.

Since hospitals were not to be trusted according to my new birthing ideologies, I wanted a home birth. Jim was somewhat on board with my childbirth and postpartum desires, but he was not open to home birth. My first birth was a semi-compromise that was not ideal, but at least I was able to realize my plan to have a natural, unmedicated birth, and have immediate and on-demand breastfeeding. This was contrary to the popular birth practices at the time, which included bottles of formula pushed on all new moms at the hospitals and having the nurses take your baby out of your room and into the nursery. I had no choice but to give birth in a hospital, which I didn't trust, so I knew I needed to be prepared for a fight.

I felt I had to keep those doctors and nurses away from my baby for fear of interference between the natural instincts of mother and child. I was able to realize some of my birthing desires for all of my births, but I still felt I wanted to do more. My natural, homegrown reality was tough, and it was often isolating.

I brought my fourth baby, Celia, home to the four acre farm on the hill outside Murphysboro, Illinois, with my three young boys, housework, gardening, car pools, part-time job, and busy husband, trying desperately to keep it all balanced. There wasn't much help from our families. My mother couldn't help me except for a day or two with a couple of the babies, and I had no mother-in-law nearby. Friends were a constant on the phone, but they were busy, too. After each birth, Jim usually had to go back to work right away (paternity leave was not a thing yet). I often thought of the cultures I had read of and romanticized whose traditions and practices honored women, infants, and birth with much more respect, and ideally gave time to nurture mother and baby. I yearned for that.

According to Donna Walls in "The Fourth Trimester," some cultures, such as in Korea, provide "the hundred days of birth," which is the resting period and pampering of the mother, baby, and the birth family. Some in Japan and China recognize similar traditions, with three weeks or a month of lovely "peace and quiet and pampering" for mother, baby, and family. Walls discusses some cultural practices throughout Africa where family takes care of mother, baby, and family for up to three months, as well. I realize this reporting does not recognize the totality of all women's experience in cultures that are outside of what I know well, but my reading of them triggered something in me. How I envied the system of taking care of postpartum mothers and babies and honoring their recovery. I wondered how our Western culture wore its arrogance of superiority without checking out how neglectful it was in treating women and infants with such disregard. We still have one of the lowest rates of maternity leave allowance in the developed world, and culturally, I don't think we have improved much in supporting mothers and families during the early postpartum time.

In addition to my birthing desires, I had very specific goals for how to feed my children. Prior to and during my childbearing years, babies were bottle-fed by the new scientifically produced, mass-marketed, Big-Business formula companies, and breast-feeding was not considered as good for baby. Individualism and stoic American values seemingly governed the practice of isolating the babies in their own cribs, in their own rooms, toughening them up for their strong individual identities.

I was determined to breastfeed my children because I believed it was the best nutrition for babies, but also because I wanted that bond. It took a Herculean effort with my first baby, Sam, to make it through the struggles of exclusively breast-feeding on my own with no back-up formula, cereal, etc. I had many people challenging my breastfeeding plans, such as a good-intentioned neighbor who brought me over a birth present for Sam: a syringe-type device to force-feed a formula/cereal mixture so the newborn would "sleep through the night." I was appalled because I wanted to be with my baby, not separated from him. I felt that a newborn sleeping twelve hours straight could be detrimental to our relationship. What bonding would I miss? This "artificial" feeding was not natural from my research of "naturalistic" societies, and so I made breastfeeding work by sheer will. I had no other choices that I could or would take in terms of formula supplements, solid food, water, or pumping/expressing. I did try pumping, but had no resources except a stupid, ineffective hand pump. I received some help from WIC (Women, Infants, and Children) for food to supplement my diet, and I was grateful for the woman who told me about the program. I had to make breastfeeding work.

My grandmother told me, when she saw my first baby for the first time, that his colic was because my breast milk was bad. (He cried inconsolably for the first six to eight weeks each day for three to four hours.) This opinion seemed very strange and ill-placed to me, and I wondered if my family felt compelled to share such misinformation because they felt rejected by me. I'm sure my generational arrogance was transparent. This upset me very much at the time.

I am glad that I endured breastfeeding despite the negativity from the older women in my family, but I have had to understand my biases and be in solidarity with the mothers and women who have had more trouble than I did. I tried to help a woman out when I was aligned for a short time with La Leche League, a breastfeeding support group, in southern Illinois.

This woman's baby had a cleft palate, and when I didn't know what to do to advise her, I had her go to the local head of the group. The leader kept advising the new mother to keep nursing and eventually the baby ended up in the hospital with dehydration. After this and other observations, I had to accept that sometimes breastfeeding works and sometimes the best efforts have to be in a compromise to account for the complexities of nutritional, emotional, and family dynamics.

After having my children, my husband and I made the choice that I would stay home as long as possible after they were each born as long as we could survive, financially. At the time, there were very few to no concessions made for mothers returning to work. I chose to be poor so I could nurture my children in the ideology that made most sense to me, and because I didn't have a situation of compromise that I could find. I nursed in public in a toilet stall, or in other places shut away doing what was, at the time, considered vulgar to many Americans.

I had been militant about being a maverick and pioneer to women by my work as a technical repair person when I worked for Xerox during my college gap year, but I was drawn to academia and art when I returned. Consequently, I could not find my way in a career or work life. I couldn't resolve my desire to be an at-home mom and still survive financially. It was a choice of taking WIC food coupons and public housing to allow me to be at home as long as possible for the four babies. I went to grad school when my first was fifteen-months-old because the stipend was better than any part time job I could get. I sewed some of his clothes from my old clothes or donated fabric. I tried odd jobs here and there, but inevitably, I just really wanted to be at home taking care of my child and my home life. I wanted to be the natural mom, gardening, canning, making bread, home schooling, etc. I tried my best and did as much as possible to provide with our little income, but it was incredibly labor intensive to make ends meet, and we moved often to make better opportunities for Jim and his work, and to find livable housing. We created as much stability as we could, but my career was never realized in a way that allowed a good income or future retirement options.

Now, I am nearly at retirement age. I loved most every moment of my babies' time when nursing, diapering, snuggling, and growing. I can still smell their baby-ness and remember freezing the moments in my memory. And I have conveniently willed away the tough memories. What I have not willed away, however, is the success I feel in having created my own birth, feeding, and parenting ideologies and remaining true to them despite consistent criticism. The reason I was able to do this was grit, first and foremost, but also by finding a community of women who actively supported each other in like-minded philosophies of birth and infant care. This took some time to locate and nurture, but progressively I was able to find my tribe. Because I stayed true to my beliefs and had the support of this community, I had four unmedicated births and developed loving relationships with each child. I was able to fall in love with my children gradually throughout the pregnancy and following their birth, and I remember looking into those wide, curious eyes as each of my beautiful babies experienced their first moments out of the womb, rooting around instinctively for the breast. Each was unique, of course, and each bonding was different, but I do remember the energy of a newborn brought into a loving and warm circle of a non-emergency, natural birth (even while recognizing how this was very fortunate and not completely in my control). I recall being cognizant that bonding and falling in love with my newborn was a process, and as we both recovered from the birth, we would find our way. It was to me a gift and a treasure of such importance.

My Favorite Part of the Day

By Laura Moore

I have what many would call a perfect life. I'm happily married with two healthy little boys, the oldest almost three years old and the youngest almost three weeks old. This is everything I've ever dreamed of. However, my favorite part of the day has nothing to do with my perfect family. In fact, it has everything to do with escaping them. What do I look forward to everyday? My twenty minutes of undivided time in the shower. And here are the top five reasons why:

Just Me

As I sit here writing this with one hand on my phone because my sweet little babe does not like to be put down, I think about the personal time I no longer have. I knew this was coming; I've been down this road once before. I love every single hour of cuddling I get with my baby and I love that he can't run away from my kisses like my Big can, but sometimes I feel trapped. Trapped in the mom-life of changing diapers, wiping noses, and keeping two humans alive. So, my twenty minutes of steamy-hot silence is all about me. I don't have to think about anything if I don't want to. I don't have to be asked to get a snack or a drink or bounce around the house with a screaming newborn or make a bottle or make dinner or wash dishes. I don't have to hear any crying or whining unless it's my own. It is my sanctuary.

Reflection and Giving Thanks

Most people pray before bed. When my baby goes to sleep, there is nothing I can think about doing besides falling asleep as fast as possible before he wants to eat again. Really, my goal is to beat him to sleep. My time in the shower is a great time for me to thank God for my amazing boys and my perfect world since I am incapable of doing it any other time of the day.

I also like to think over my day. Some days are better than others and it is important to reflect. My husband has a busy job and there is always an upcoming holiday, so it's nice to just have time to think. The water just gives me the clarity I need to be a stable person when I exit the shower and re-enter mom-life.

Crazy Hormones

My first few postpartum weeks home were a hot mess. Literally. I would freeze all day and sweat uncontrollably all night. For some reason, I would shiver and be insanely cold in the evening. I couldn't wait to get in the shower just to be warm—before I started to sweat again. I felt physically good in the shower when I didn't feel good at any other time. It was medicine.

The Calm Before the Nighttime Storm

Anyone with a newborn usually dreads the night. It's kind of lonely and can seem endless. Somehow, taking a hot shower relieves a little bit of the anxiety of the coming night. I know these nights won't last forever, especially since I already forgot about the nights with my three-year-old son. In the moment though, this does not seem temporary. When I am able to have my shower meditation, I can better handle whatever sleeplessness that might lie ahead.

I Stink

What people neglect to tell women is how much they might stink postpartum. Between the hormones, sweating, blood, dried vomit, and tears, that momma stank is potent! Twenty minutes a day in the shower probably isn't enough time to combat this, but it's a good start.

So there, my friends, are my top five reasons I look forward to a hot shower all day long. Twenty minutes away from reality is a daily necessity for everyone, and the shower provides an excellent place to become human again.

Big Moment

by Abby Spears

When I was nineteen, one of my favorite shows on TV was *One Tree Hill*. The show was full of teenage angst and melodrama and every character was basically a supermodel. Tucked away in each episode was a tiny life lesson that actually applied to the real world; this was the best part. My favorite quote from the show is, "There are only a few moments in life where you can look back later and say to yourself, 'That's when it all changed.'" I had been looking for my own personal "moment" that would spark life-altering changes. Little did I know, that moment was right around the corner.

My sophomore year of college had been a difficult year. One week before I was to move back into my dorm, a good friend was killed in an accidental fire caused by his college roommates. I barely had time to process the visitation and funeral before it was time to pack up and move to Illinois State University for the year. I had experienced the deaths of two grandfathers in elementary school, but this death was untimely. My friend wasn't old and hadn't lived a long, fulfilling life. He wasn't going to experience adulthood like the rest of us, and it felt wrong that we were still here. I thought this was one of my Moments. I thought, "Damn. Life is just going to continue like this, and then we're all going to die. What's the point in trying to be happy or have fun when all the people I love are just going to die?" Food stopped sounding good, music stopped making me want to dance, and movies could no longer captivate me. My joy from life's little pleasures had been sapped.

Once the school year was over and summer vacation was just beginning, I vowed to get back to some sort of normalcy. I worked part-time and babysat. Between my two jobs and try-ing to find time for my friends and boyfriend, I really had no time to be sad or angry, which was exactly what I needed. After being in such a deep depression from my young friend's death, the distraction of work was even allowing me to start feeling hungry again. Once, while babysitting, the kids re-quested macaroni and cheese for lunch. I made a whole box and served them, then ate the leftovers myself. When I was finished I was still starving, which was abnormal for me, so I made an entire second box. The kids were already full and were back to playing with their toys, so I sat and ate the entire second box by myself. Curious. A few days later, the little girl was playing with her "big girl purse" and I asked her to show it to me. She had a blast taking all of her trinkets out of the purse and explaining them to me. She even had her own mint lip gloss. She waved it in my face a few times and the mint scent was so strong that I gagged, and had to run to the bathroom to dry-heave a few times. Even more curious. I chalked it up to my two stomach ulcers.

The weekend before the Fourth of July, my friends had organized a huge get-together with all of our high school friends who were around for the summer. Typically at parties, I was the "mom" and remained sober so that I could ensure my friends were safe. I never enjoyed the feeling of being drunk and was always paranoid about date-rape drugs after all the episodes of *Law & Order* I had seen. Additionally, I had a controlling and verbally abusive boyfriend who didn't approve of me getting drunk when I wasn't under his watch. For some reason, at this particular party, I decided to drink. I had a couple shots of vodka and a tiny, and weak, mixed drink. The party was fun and I didn't feel drunk. I figured I was golden and the next day I wouldn't feel a thing. So when I woke up feeling like the world was spinning and proceeded to throw up a couple of times, I was astonished. "Is my tolerance really that bad? Did someone put something in my drink? Why do I feel so shitty?"

Around the time of the Mysterious Hangover was when I noticed that it had been awhile since I had my period. I was never a "period tracker" with accuracy, but I was pretty regular. As I tried to work backwards to when my last period was, I realized I was late by more than a week. This had never happened to me; my cycles just always varied by two or three days at the most. Oh shit. This is bad. This is really, really bad. I turned to my go-to strategy in stressful situations: Bury. Avoid. Ignore. I waited two more days JUST IN CASE. Then I couldn't take it anymore. I Googled "pregnancy symptoms" and clicked on the first link. It listed "10 Common Pregnancy Symptoms." As I glanced down the list, I was getting more nervous. When I got to the bottom, I had nine out of the ten. Shit balls mother fucker. I quickly closed the tab and then deleted my search history in case my parents used my laptop. I knew it was time to take action, but I was scared shitless to leave my bedroom. Then my mom yelled upstairs that dinner was ready, so I took a deep breath, put on my Everything Is Fine mask, and proceeded downstairs.

Later that night, I was supposed to hang out at a friend's house but I made a few pit stops along the way. First I stopped at Walgreen's to buy a pregnancy test. As I walked up and down random aisles to make it look like I was there for more than just a pregnancy test, I began to feel as though I had a big neon sign on top of my head that said, "Pregnant Teenager." I finally dragged myself to the Family Planning aisle and swiped a box that had two tests. I made sure to pay for it using only my right hand, so that my empty left ring finger wouldn't be judged. Then I left, and drove to Schnuck's. I didn't really need to be at Schnuck's, but I invented a story in my head that my friend wanted me to bring chips and salsa when I came over. There is nothing more normal than bringing chips and salsa to your friend's house. But I unpacked one of the pregnancy tests, put it in my purse, and stopped in the bathroom at Schnuck's before picking up the food.

There I was, in a Schnuck's bathroom at 9:15pm, all by myself, peeing on a stick. Here it was: my Big Moment. I peed on the stick, hands shaking, and then set it on top of the toilet paper dispenser to wait. Two pink lines stared back at me. Two definite, dark pink lines. Holy shit. What the fuck am I going to do? I wrapped the stick in toilet paper and put it back in my purse. Then I washed my hands, bought some chips and salsa in a daze, and headed to my friend's house.

All of my close friends were already at the house so I dropped the chips and salsa onto her dining room table and said, "I brought snacks!" Literally, the next thing out of someone's mouth was, "Aww, you're such a mom!" I felt like the wind was knocked out of me. I tried to giggle but I think it came out as more of a moan. Then I grabbed Maggie, the only one of my friends who could actually keep a secret, and told her I needed to show her something in my car. No one seemed to think that was odd so she followed me out to my car. When we got there I pulled out the stick from my purse and said, "I need you to look at this and tell me what you see." Before she even saw it she said, "Oh my God, you're pregnant!" Then she actually looked at it and said, "Well, shit! Yeah, you're pregnant. But you're going to be fine. You know that right? This is going to be fine." I love her for her response. There was no judgment, no prodding or questioning, only encouragement. And that was exactly what I needed in that moment.

Parker and I had been dating for almost three years at this point, but it had never been a healthy or stable relationship. I discovered early on that he was cheating on me with multiple other people. I found out initially by showing up at his house twenty minutes earlier than he expected me. I walked into the house and his mom said he was on his computer. I turned the corner and saw him typing furiously in an AIM (AOL Instant Messenger) message. I said, "Hey! Got here earlier than I thought! Surprise!" He immediately turned on me with a look of panic, then yelled at me that I should've texted him first. It was obvious that he was trying to hide whatever was on the computer screen and when I asked him about it he got even angrier with me. He admitted it was a girl he was talking to, but claimed she was "stalking him" and he was just trying to get rid of her. He warned me to never talk to her, and that if she reached out to me that I shouldn't believe anything she said. Between him yelling at me and it dawning on me that this probably meant he was cheating on me, I got overwhelmed and emotional. He ignored me and continued typing on the screen for a while, and told me that if I was going to cry and be a baby then I needed to go home.

From then on, I was on constant alert for any notification he received on his computer or phone. Every little "ding" set off a flurry of thoughts, fears, and emotions. I would have to weigh the risk of asking him who he was talking to and then facing his wrath, or pretending everything was fine and then being awake all night wondering. In turn, he began to be suspicious of all of my activities and I allowed him to put me under constant scrutiny. He would take my phone and go through it any time he pleased. If there was a text from any male he would ask endless questions to get to the bottom of why that guy would be texting me and what I did to make that guy think I was interested in him. He would often make me sign into my AIM account on his computer so he could check my recent conversations. If a male messaged me while I was logged in then I would get screamed at, even if I didn't respond. When we would go out in public together he would constantly be in close physical contact with me in order to ward off other potential suitors. Once, I had been texting back and forth with my older male cousin, Michael, who lived in Chicago. I let Michael know about my plans to come to Chicago to see *Wicked* with my friends, and Michael let me know that he would be free before and after the play if I wanted to meet and catch up. I had to spend thirty minutes convincing my boyfriend that Michael was my cousin and not a romantic interest.

My only explanation for staying in a relationship where I was taken for granted, verbally abused, manipulated, and used for so long is that I truly felt like that was what I deserved. All of my friends hated him. My parents disapproved of him. Both of my brothers have since confessed that it was hard for them to watch me be in that relationship. However, being a nineteen year old with a tendency towards stubbornness, I refused to give up. I could make it work. He would change for me. I'm not good enough for anyone else. He barely wanted to date me so there's no way anyone else ever would. I had lost my virginity to him and I had a rose-colored vision of the world. I thought I had fallen in love with someone, but the truth is that I found someone who hated me almost as much as I hated myself.

To make my peeing-on-a-stick situation even stickier, I had just discovered Parker was still cheating on me with the girl from the computer, as well as someone else. Computer Girl and my boyfriend conducted what I call an affair, where they basically had their own weird version of a relationship alongside the relationship he and I had. He and I had the public, "real" relationship. He and Computer Girl had a cyber relationship that was deeply emotional. He confided in her more than me and often told me that she understood him better than I did. I'm not sure any physical cheating ever came to fruition, but I know they had almost daily webcam and Skype conversations that were emotional and sexual in nature. Computer Girl somehow got ahold of my AIM screen name and would randomly decide to clue me in on things they were doing or things he had done with other girls. She was the one who messaged me in early June to let me know he had hooked up with Girl On The Side. There were odd times that she felt more like an ally or a sister-wife, and we would both be like, "Yeah fuck him! He's such an asshole!" And then I would remember that this was the other person he had a relationship with and that I hated her with every fiber of my being.

On the night I was in the Schnuck's bathroom, I hadn't spoken to my boyfriend in over a week. Not knowing how long this break would last, I refrained from sharing the positive pregnancy test with him. At first he stayed away and left me alone. After the second full week he began to text me again and ask why I hadn't called or come over in so long. I replied with vague answers but found that for the first time in two years he was not my number one priority. My early pregnancy hormones were raging and my earliest maternal instinct had begun to take hold. I started realizing he was going to be a terrible dad. I knew very early on that this baby would need to be protected from him whether I kept it or gave it up for adoption. I began building up a wall of protection around myself in order to protect my future child. It wasn't a perfect setup and it was only the beginning of a long road I needed to walk, but it was a step in the right direction.

July, 2008

Slowly, I started getting the word out about my pregnancy. The only people who knew were Maggie and Eileen, a long-lost grade school friend who I still kept up with via social media. Eileen messaged me two days after I told Maggie. She told me she got married to her boyfriend even though they were both only nineteen and wanted advice on how to deal with her mom's disapproval. I replied to her message with a bombshell of my own and asked her advice in return on how to deal with my mom's future disapproval. (Fun Fact: She is still happily married.) I figured Eileen was a safe person to tell because I could type my answer rather than say it out loud, and we had known each other since we were six. We went to different high schools and had completely separate friend groups so there was no chance of people finding out through the grapevine. Next, I decided to tell my three best friends from high school. I knew I needed to do it over the phone and that I should probably have some sort of speech prepared that I could just rattle off. I've never been a fan of "winging it" and now was not the time to start.

The first friend I called was Benny. Benny had gone through quite a rebellious streak since she left for Eastern Illinois University, and she responded with jubilance. She immediately wanted to start discussing baby clothes, baby shoes, and strollers. I had to pump the breaks and let her know that I still hadn't officially decided to keep the baby, even though I was pretty sure that was what I would do. She stopped asking about going shopping for baby stuff, but she never stopped being excited. Benny was the friend who tended to tell you what you wanted to hear, but I think most of her excitement was genuine. She was a great friend to "break the ice" with and get the first phone call out of the way.

The second friend I called was Chloe. She responded with grave concern for me. She asked questions like, "How are you sleeping? Have you been sick at all?" and "Is there anything I can do for you?" I told her over and over that for now I was ok, but she reassured me she would be a shoulder to cry on if I needed one. She did eventually ask if I had decided to keep the baby, and I told her almost but not quite. She understood and didn't press any further. Chloe's empathy was the most touching of the responses I received.

The third friend I told was Anya. She was always the most reserved of our friends and in hindsight her reaction was predictable. I called her and spilled my well-rehearsed guts. When I finished talking, there was dead silence on the other end of the line for at least five seconds. Then her first words were, "Well... I will say some prayers for you." She eventually asked if I had told my parents yet and also if I had spoken to my priest. My answer to both of those questions was, "No," which was met with more silence on her end. What I didn't realize when I hung up was that phone call sparked the end of our friendship.

I was starting to experience morning sickness, except it was all-day sickness, and it was getting harder to hide behind my "ulcers acting up" excuse. I knew I needed to get to a doctor and make sure everything was healthy, but I had never been to a gynecologist before so I needed my mom's help to set that up. And I needed to figure out what I was going to do about school. After a rough sophomore year at ISU, I had applied and gotten into the same program at the University of Illinois. I had registered for courses, attended orientation, cosigned on a lease for an apartment, and stocked up on Illini gear. But five weeks before move-in day I was in my bedroom writing a letter to my mom that I was roughly six weeks pregnant and that I was terribly sorry for the great disappointment I knew I was.

My dad was at work so I put the letter into a box with both of the positive pregnancy tests and set it on her side of their bed. I walked downstairs to find her in the living room and told her I had put something in her room for her. I followed her upstairs but went to my own room instead. I laid on my bed with my teddy bear and forgot to breathe until she came in to find me a few minutes later. She had big crocodile tears streaming down her face, but she hugged me for a long time and didn't say anything. Once we let go she asked if I was ok, and I replied, "yes, kind of, I think so." I remember saying, "Please don't tell Dad yet," and she agreed not quite yet but soon we would have to tell him. At some point we moved from my bedroom to hers, and she called her OB/GYN to get me in as soon as possible.

They had an available appointment to do bloodwork later that afternoon, so I took it. She drove me to the appointment and I vaguely remember getting my blood drawn. I felt shaky again just like I had when I was in the Schnuck's bathroom, and I wanted to tell them they didn't need to do a stupid blood test to confirm what I already knew. Being in a stark white doctor's office with the smell of hand sanitizer all around made me come to terms with my reality in a way that I had not yet experienced. My life as a "normal" nineteen-year-old college student was effectively over, and everything I would experience from now on would be through a lens that most of my peers wouldn't have until many years down the road, if ever.

We drove home in relative silence, with a tentative sonogram appointment set up for one week later, pending the bloodwork results. My mom is a nervous driver on a normal day, and that day she was really white-knuckling it. When we got home she got me settled into her room, because it had a TV, and asked if I needed anything to eat or drink. I said no because I was kind of nauseous. Then she sat down and said, "You know I need you to tell me who the father of this baby is." I referenced my handwritten note and told her I was too embarrassed and that I didn't want him to be involved anyway. She said, "I already have a pretty good idea of who it is though, I just need you to confirm it." So then I did confirm that yes, my asshole of an ex-boyfriend who used and abused me for the previous three years was, in fact, the father of this child. She let out a big breath and then without missing a beat said, "Do NOT marry him. This does not mean you two need to get married. I don't want you to EVER think that your dad and I feel that just because you're having a baby together you should get married." I told her that I had no intention of even telling him I was pregnant, let alone marrying him. She seemed relieved at that, but then she reminded me that we would need to tell my dad when he got home from work. I cried but agreed with her. She left me up there with my TV shows and my teddy bear and went downstairs to hang out with my brothers, who were blissfully ignorant.

My mom told my dad before they came upstairs to find me. When he came into the room he was already crying and he didn't say a word; he just hugged me. After we let go I said I was sorry and he shook his head, still crying, and said, "Don't be. This is family. This is what we do together." Then he told me he was so sorry that I had to go through this by myself. He had watched his older brother and one of his nieces go through pregnancies out of wedlock when he was growing up and he told me he knew firsthand that it would be hard, but that it was something we could all get through together. I felt relieved and comforted, but then my mom's phone rang and it was the doctor. She answered and talked for a minute but I couldn't tell what was being discussed. When she hung up she explained that the bloodwork was already back and that it was showing that I was pregnant, but that it was very early on and my levels weren't very high yet. They kept the sono appointment for one week out and said I would have to wait until then to get more solid answers. So my feelings of relief were quickly replaced with more feelings of limbo. What do I do with myself for a whole week? Do I need to call U of I and drop my fall classes? What about the apartment I signed a lease for with my friends? Am I going to be able to support a child on a teacher's salary or should I change my major?

Together with my parents, I figured out the answer to all of those questions over the next week while we waited for the sonogram. We decided that I should pull out of U of I for the year. I would need to try to find a subleaser for the apartment and that I should only change my major if it was something I wanted to do for myself. Calling the registrar at U of I and withdrawing my enrollment was a much harder phone call than I thought it would be. I cried for a long time when I hung up, and then I packed up all of the fun Illini gear I had been collecting throughout the spring and put it away in a box at the back of my closet. Since I hadn't gotten into U of I my freshman year I was thrilled and proud to be transferring there my junior year. It would take me five years to be able to dig that box out and go through it without crying. I decided to change my major from Elementary Education to Secondary Education with a concentration in Family & Consumer Sciences. During the year of my pregnancy, I decided I would attend a junior college to get caught up on courses and stay on my dad's insurance plan. I planned on transferring to Bradley University to finish my degree the following fall. I had been working at the mall, and when they found out I would be staying around for the school year, they offered to make me a part-time manager, which came with a raise. By the end of that week of limbo, I was feeling a little more in control of my future.

I was starting to experience more intense morning sickness, or rather, all day sickness. At first it was just a touch of nausea and I could blame it on all the stress I was going through. But by the end of the week, I was experiencing multiple sessions of vomiting per day with severe nausea. It was hard to keep food down, which only made me more nauseous. I went to my sonogram with a puke bowl just in case. My mom drove me there and stayed with me the whole time. I had no idea until the moment I was laying spread-eagle on the bed that the first sonogram is done "internally," which means they stick a dildo-shaped camera up your lady parts with some lube and poke around in there for about ten minutes. The sono tech quickly found my growing baby and confirmed what we already knew: I was about seven weeks pregnant. She asked a lot of questions about the last time I ovulated and when I last had a cycle and about when I think I conceived, and I mumbled through explanations about how I didn't know I was supposed to track any of those things. They sent me home with several photos of what looked like one tiny grain of rice inside a circle, and helped me make my next several appointments. I felt like I had jumped over a hurdle and then realized I had one hundred more hurdles to go.

My mom had been nagging me about when and how I would tell Parker I was pregnant. I kept insisting that I was never going to tell him and my mom, who was a therapist, kept telling me that was avoidant behavior and it was not a good coping mechanism. As it turned out, no matter how hard I could have tried to avoid telling him, it would have done me no good. I was shopping in JC Penney looking for big, flowy shirts to wear down the road as my belly grew, when I started receiving phone calls from him. I ignored the first few, but after six or seven calls in a row I figured he wasn't going to give up. I barely got out my, "Hello?" when he laid into me. He was screaming at the top of his lungs that he couldn't believe I would go and get myself pregnant and then not have the guts to tell him about it. I think every other customer in JC Penney could hear him and was now fully aware of my business. I quickly tried to exit the store and get outside so no one else could hear. Once outside, I found a bench to sit on and tried to take some calming breaths. After he got done ranting at me I was silent until he said, "WELL???? You ARE pregnant aren't you?!?!" I quietly said, "Yes," then tried to ask how in the world he had found out, but he had already launched into another attack. He got through his second rant and I finally got to ask how he found out. He casually replied that Computer Girl had hacked into my social media and read my personal messages back and forth to my friend Eileen. He was completely calm as he read word-for-word the exchange between Eileen and me as if this was normal. He then demanded to know who this Eileen was and why I was telling her my business. Inside my head I was infuriated and wanted to scream. How in the world was any of this my fault? Number one: I hadn't simply "gotten my-self" pregnant. Number two: no wonder I hadn't told him yet. Number three: how in the name of Jesus, Mary, and Joseph did this bitch HACK INTO MY MYSPACE? But the abused girlfriend went into autopilot and I apologized that I hadn't told him sooner. I assured him that I wouldn't ask for child support and I would do this all on my own, that it was noth-ing he needed to worry about. He calmed down after that and said some weird stuff like, "Maybe this could be exciting," and "You have to come over so we can tell my parents." I tried to say no, but within a few days he guilted me into going to his house to sit down with his parents to share the news.

My parents didn't know I was going to his house. I was too ashamed to admit that he had found out and had then guilted me into spending time with him. When I arrived at his house, his mom clearly already knew everything. She was absolutely giddy and was smiling ear-to-ear. His older sister had just recently had a baby, and his mom was thrilled to be a grandma again. Seeing her act this way made me feel physically ill, even more than I already did with morning sickness. She kept reassuring both of us that we would be great "mommies and daddies." My internal voice was screaming, "Run! Get out!" But externally, I smiled and nodded. His dad was more serious and accusatory. He spent a lot of time putting on a show and trying to lecture his son about how he needed to be a good father to this child. It was all bullshit. He liked to stroke his own ego and make himself seem like a good dad by giving his son these lectures from time to time, but they were always without merit. He had a shitty son because he was married to a piece of shit and they were shitty parents. After an hour of awkward conversation with the three of them, I made an excuse to leave. My boyfriend/ex-boyfriend walked me to my car with his hands all over me and tried to kiss me. When I denied him and explained that we were still broken up, he got defensive and tried to intimidate me by saying something like, "You couldn't find anyone better than me before this and you're definitely not going to get anyone better now." I quickly got in my car and drove away but cried the whole way home, because he had just said out loud what I had feared most since the moment I saw those two pink lines.

August, 2008

It was the Beijing Olympics, and Michael Phelps had just won his eighth gold medal in a row. I felt so connected to him in that moment, because I had just vomited for the eighth time in a row. I don't remember much about this month aside from laying on the couch, binge watching lots of Olympics and Bravo shows, and puking my guts out. There were several times I had to leave work because I couldn't stop throwing up. No food ever sounded good and I usually resorted to plain rice or plain mashed potatoes at the end of the night. I couldn't keep down the prenatal vitamins to save my life and I lost several pounds. The doctor became concerned that I wasn't getting enough nutrients. He finally wrote me a prescription for medication that did the trick, sort of. As long as I took my nausea medicine within ten minutes of waking up, I could function on low-speed until 11:15am. That was the magic time of day that I felt a little bit human again, until 8:00 at night when it all started over. I continued trying to take the prenatal vitamins for a week after I got the nausea medicine but it was still difficult to keep them down. After a week of failing to keep vitamins in my body, I never took another one. I felt guilty that I wasn't making more of an effort to nourish my growing baby, but I was in survival mode, and those pills were a huge obstacle.

October, 2008

As fall semester began, so did my second trimester. On the first day of all my new classes, I stayed after class to introduce myself to each professor and inform them of my "condition." By October, I had gotten into a routine of seeing similar people day-to-day and didn't feel like I was constantly having to explain my "situation" to new people. It still felt very much like a "situation" to me and I never got to a point where I was confident that everything was going to turn out successfully. However, it was around this time that I developed a mental shield around myself that helped me cope with stress. I was never harassed or shamed in public for being pregnant out of wedlock at a young age, but I'm the type of person that takes on a lot of shame even when it's not being explicitly directed at me. I would pay close attention to nonverbal cues from everyone

I met as to whether or not they were silently judging me, and many times I thought they were. I could have been wrong, but I needed to protect myself all the same. My shield was made of self-deprecating humor, and my theory was that if I made fun of myself first then it wouldn't be as funny if someone else made fun of me later. Before this time in my life, I had been far too insecure to poke fun at myself and I became overly sensitive if others poked fun at me. But now it was a way for me to connect with people, break the ice, and talk about the elephant in the room. When my friend introduced me to her new boyfriend, I told him, "By the way don't worry, I'm not obese, I'm just pregnant." Later she told me that he thought that was the funniest thing because I was more worried about him judging my weight than my pregnancy. Deep down the opposite was true, but by throwing out my one-liner I had made them both think the tables were turned.

The end of October brought my big gender reveal sonogram and the halfway point of my pregnancy. In 2008, there was no such thing as a Gender Reveal Party; there was just a sonogram and then you went about your business. I knew in my soul from very early in the pregnancy that I was carrying a girl. It was an instinctual phenomenon that took over my senses and convinced me that this baby just HAD to be a girl. Prior to my sonogram, I had narrowed my name search down to three names. I was stuck between two girl names, and I chose a boy name just in case. I drove myself to my appointment and waited patiently while she poked around my belly, measuring head circumference and heart ventricles. Then she said it was time to look at the gender and asked if I wanted to find out. "YES!" I replied, and then held my breath. She looked from three different angles and then said, "I have a very good guess, let me just check from one more angle." A minute later she confirmed my notion that yes, in fact, I was carrying a girl. I believe I said something like, "It's time for there to be a girl in my life. I grew up with two brothers and they're smelly and loud." By the time I drove myself home I had made my final decision on her name: Jocelyn. It means happy and joyful. Her middle name would be James, because that is my dad and brother's middle names, and she would have my last name, Swanson. In that moment I steeled myself for the backlash that was sure to come but I was ready to defend my decision.

I am certain his mother made him call. We had spoken maybe twice since we told his parents I was pregnant. He was still feeling salty that I had denied him access to my body as he had walked me to my car that day. Normally, that was a trick that would work on me, but now that I had someone besides myself to protect, it was been easy to keep my guard up. The day of my sonogram, he didn't text the usual, "What's up?" He just called out of the blue. He also knew that it was the exact day I had found out the gender of the baby. For a guy who always had trouble remembering my birthday, this seemed fishy. I told him it was a girl and of course he asked if I had decided on a name. I told him I had decided on Jocelyn James. I didn't explain any of my reasoning because I didn't have to. This was my decision and mine alone. He got quiet when he noticed I was being short with him and he tried to make awkward small talk. I thought I was in the clear and maybe I could get off the phone without him bringing up the last name, but no such luck. He snuck the question in and I replied, "She's going to have my last name." He was again quiet and I braced myself for a loud verbal assault, but it never came. He remained quiet and simply asked why. I explained that I was the one carrying her, I was going to give birth to her, and I was going to raise her every minute of every day for the rest of my life. I asked if he could honestly say the same for himself. He remained quiet and then started trying to make it seem like he was crying, so I made an excuse and hung up. Three hours later I got a phone call from his mother. She was using her super-sugary-sweet voice and went on and on about how excited she was that the baby was a girl and that now she would have both a girl and a boy "grandbaby." Then she dug into her real reason for calling. She wanted to know why I had chosen a name for the baby without talking to her son at all. I explained that we had only talked twice since July and that he seemed to be carrying on with his life just fine, and that this pregnancy was not affecting his decisions or life-path the way it was affecting mine. She then switched to her pouty voice and told me how I had really hurt his feelings and that he had spent a lot of time coming up with a name that he liked but when I didn't even ask if he had names in mind that he got very depressed. I held my ground and reasserted myself, so then she tried another tactic. She launched into a seven minute monologue where I couldn't get a word in edgewise. The gist of her speech was that no matter how hard I tried to keep this baby away from them it was still part of their family too and they had just as much right to love her as I did. That I was going to do my daughter an injustice if I kept their family hidden from her and it would damage her in the long run. When she finally finished, I reminded her that I had never and would never intend to keep the baby away from them, but that I was simply taking on the responsibility of naming my child the way I had taken on the responsibility of carrying her, giving birth to her, and raising her. I reminded her that her son had only texted to check in on me twice, had never come to spend time with me or the baby, and had not been to a single doctor's appointment, thus far. She assured me that would change soon because he was so distraught by my hostility that he was going to prove it to me that he cared for the baby as much as I did. I finally got off the phone with her and felt emotionally exhausted. But a sense of pride washed over me at the same time because I didn't feel like I needed to fly to his side to fix everything, even though he was in distress.

December, 2008

The same battles were ensuing between Parker, his mom, and me, but they had taken on different forms. First, I was supposed to be inviting him to doctor's appointments, and if I wasn't then I was purposely excluding him. Second, I was supposed to let her throw a shower for me with their side of the family even though he and I weren't back together. Third, I was supposed to make time for their family during the holidays, even though I was still pregnant, and I would have to make more time for them next year once the baby was here. With each battle, I stood my ground the best I could, but the third trimester fatigue left me feeling physically and emotionally drained. My parents supported all the boundaries I set for him and his family, but enforcing those boundaries was exhausting. There were times I faltered because I'm human and I was also full of pregnancy hormones. I continued going to doctor appointments by myself and I refused to attend a shower with their family. However, I did break down during the holidays and attend one Christmas party with him. His mom insisted that he had picked out a gift for the baby all on his own but I knew it was a lie. I kind of just wanted them to stay off my back for a while and I figured going to this dumb party and opening a stupid present would do the trick. The rest of the evening passed in an awkward blur. When I tried to leave, Parker followed me out to my car. This was his way of trying to find "alone time" where he could work his manipulative magic on me and make me miss him. He said something like, "So you're really over me this time then?" and added a pouty face and slouched posture. I explained that I was very confused as to why he was upset about me moving on when he was the one who had been hanging out with different girls every weekend and living up the party scene all this time. He tried to explain it away with the same old excuses: "Those girls don't matter," and "I have to keep up my reputation with the boys. I can't just stop showing up at parties," but it all sounded so bizarre from my new vantage point. I tried to explain to him how strange his reasoning sounded but it fell on deaf ears. He was getting visibly upset and I knew a rampage would soon be unleashed, so I quickly got in my car and drove away. He called several times later that night but I never answered, and he finally dropped the issue for several weeks.

December was also filled with many holiday gatherings with my extended family. By this time everyone knew I was pregnant and was accepting of the situation. They all showed me support in numerous ways. I grew up in a large Catholic family that always rallied around each other in times of need, but I had never been the specific rallying point before. I was one of twenty-nine grandchildren and until then had never appreciated how lucky I was to be in such a loving, devoted family. The way each of them showed true, genuine care for me helped put things in perspective. They asked how I was doing and then actually listened to my answer. They brought me gently used baby clothes from their own children. They only gave advice when I asked for it. They knew how to have a conversation with me without making me feel like I was under a microscope. I started seeing that THIS was how a family operated, out of selflessness, and that made for a stark contrast to the way I was treated by Parker and his family. Spending quality time with my large family over the holidays helped remind me that I was not going through this alone.

January, 2009

The Year of Jocelyn was upon me. I was no longer carrying a fetus; I was carrying a baby that was going to show up very soon. I was going to have to adjust my entire lifestyle to this brand new human. I was never going to be able to just sit and read *Harry Potter* by myself, or watch reruns of *The Fresh Prince of Bel Air* on a lazy Sunday. All of these thoughts terrified me. But I tried to remind myself that there would be things to look forward to along the way. For one, all of my friends had planned to throw me a baby shower. For another, my mom and I were finalizing the nursery decorations. The shower was beautiful and all of my friends from high school, college, and work were there. They spoiled me with tons of gifts and plenty of tiny clothes and shoes. My mom and I had fun putting away all the pretty outfits, organizing the diapers and bottles, and deciding where the baby furniture would fit best in her nursery. We painted the walls to look like a garden in a Monet painting and hung up matching curtains. I began putting together a scrapbook of images from my pregnancy to share with my daughter in the future. Most of the photos were from the fall and included Halloween, Thanksgiving, and Christmas pictures. I had carefully chosen outfits for all three of those holidays and my little bump looked adorable even though it was causing me discomfort in real life. After developing the film from my shower and seeing how prominent my bump had become, I decided not to add any photos of myself pregnant after that date. The last two months of pregnancy brought aches, pains, and tenderness that I did not want to remember.

February, 2009

By the middle of February, all of the fun events were over and I was just a beached whale who was barely making it from her car to her college classes without needing an oxygen tank. My junior college's parking lot was deceivingly far away from the buildings, no matter which building a class might be in.

My winter coat no longer buttoned, my shoes had all stretched out to accommodate my swollen feet, and I was rotating three pairs of pants because that was all that fit. In early February, I took a Lamaze class with my mom and that was one of the worst ideas I'd ever had. Everyone else in the class was there with an ultra-planned pregnancy and their doting husband in tow. They already had typed Birth Plans and many were fans of "going natural," without any drugs to aid in delivery. I had no husband and no Birth Plan, and I basically planned on asking the doctor to give me as many drugs as possible. The class did help me brush up on some breathing techniques that I used while I was in labor, but that was the only benefit. I had seen birth videos before, but seeing them in this Lamaze class scared the crap out of me because now I knew that all of those things were actually going to happen to me and my poor vagina. My mom tried to soothe my anxiety during these classes, and that was a very sweet gesture, but she really only made it worse. When she would try to give helpful hints or rub my back, I kept thinking that this was just another example of how my pregnancy was not "normal" or "traditional." Instead of a husband rubbing my shoulders and soothing my fears, I had my mom there mothering me while I prepared to be a mother myself.

How could I be a mother if I still needed my mom to mother me? That question was a mantra that began playing itself over and over in my mind and made me increasingly more anxious the nearer my due date was. I started panicking and feeling as though I was not ready for the enormous amount of responsibility that was about to be placed on me, and me alone.

Years later, I would come to understand that the last month of pregnancy is when hormones start to shift back to the pre-pregnancy state, and the early signs of postpartum depression can set in as early as six weeks before delivery. But without that knowledge, all I understood was that a sense of foreboding and dread had settled throughout my entire body. I began having thoughts that were completely irrational but that made total sense to me at the time. I was certain that I would never be able to date anyone or get married because I had somehow gained sixty pounds during this pregnancy and my body was wrecked. Therefore, this was bound to be the only child I would ever have. The general public would only see my daughter and me as a stereotype: a spoiled Only Child being raised by a Single Mother. I was determined to overcome that stereotype and started holding myself to an extremely high standard of perfection, both personally and as a mom. I became obsessed with projecting an image of myself that did not match up with who I really was on the inside. To the world, I was tackling this hurdle with strength and dignity, but privately I doubted myself constantly. I felt like the most incompetent human alive. I still relied on my parents for housing, food, clothing, and college tuition. If I couldn't take on any of those responsibilities myself there was no way I could successfully raise another person. I had made the mistake of letting the most narcissistic and controlling asshole get me pregnant and now the entire world knew about my darkest secret. I had lost my virginity to him and was struggling to move past the trauma he had caused me. There was a chance my daughter would inherit some of his characteristics and I would be dealing with someone who treated me as terribly as he had for the rest of my life.

Additionally, Parker and his mother were now forcing their way into my life on a more consistent basis. The closer my due date got, the more "involved" they pretended to be. I gained an appreciation for how easy it had been to stand up to them when they kept themselves at a distance versus how hard it was now that they were a constant presence. He demanded to be in the room when I gave birth because he claimed it was his right, and he tried to get me to allow his mother in the room, as well. I drew the line with her, but told him he could be there. I tried to warn him this would mean he would need to be readily available at any given moment, whether he was busy partying or with another girl. He said that wouldn't be a problem and made me feel like I was overreacting, because of course the birth of his daughter would come first and foremost. Meanwhile, my family was having a hard time accepting my decision to let him be in the birth room. My parents had patiently and lovingly supported me for the past eight months. They never complained about any extra costs or how much stress we were all under. I completely understood their frustration with him forcing his way in, and I internalized most of that frustration. I still entrusted the most important tasks to my parents when I typed up my Birth Plan. My dad was in charge of keeping track of my overnight bag, my pillow, and my teddy bear. He was also responsible for calling everyone on my list when the baby was born. My mom was going to be my partner during labor and delivery and would help me make major decisions if something went wrong.

March, 2009

Jocelyn Month was finally here. I was an even bigger beached whale, still waddling back and forth to classes and up and down the aisles at work. I started getting some super interesting comments in public, as all first-time mothers do. Many people wanted to make sure, really sure, that I was only having one baby because it sure looked like twins. One customer at the store literally poked me in the belly, without asking, and said, "Woop! Your turkey baster popped! Won't be long now!" Lots of old women thought I really needed to hear the horror stories of their niece's best friend's neighbor when she gave birth. These little tidbits worked wonders for the mounting depression and anxiety that was coming to a full swell. I was already insecure about my weight, so the comments about twins were terrifying. And I was petrified of the pain I was about to go through during labor and delivery. Luckily, all the women in my family were constantly checking in on me and making sure I was coping. I would often joke with several of my aunts about how there should be a Rule Book written for the general public on things you can and can't say to a pregnant lady. I even got a few phone calls from my uncles and cousins checking on me and making sure I was handling the upcoming changes ok. All of these kind and caring gestures stood in stark contrast to the message I was getting from Parker and his family. They would only call to verify that I hadn't changed my mind and that they would still be included in the birth experience. They reminded me that even though I wasn't going to let his parents be in the birth room, they would be waiting right outside with their family. They showed no care or concern for me or the baby, only about the attention they would get once they had a baby to show off.

March 15, 2009

I do not have any horror stories and my birth went as well as expected from a medical standpoint. I woke up on Saturday, March 14th, realizing that my mucus plug had made an appearance all over my sheets overnight. I told my mom about it and she said not to worry, that it would still be awhile before anything crazy happened. I spent the day being lazy and watching TV. A couple of my friends stopped by to hang out that afternoon, and I noticed that I was having contractions about every twenty minutes while they were there. All evening the contractions continued to be about twenty minutes apart. We ate pizza for dinner, and by 8:00pm they were ten minutes apart. At around 10:00, my mom suggested getting in a hot shower to speed up the contractions. That did the trick, and after a long shower they were six to seven minutes apart. I paced back and forth in the living room watching *Coming to America* for the next hour to see if they would speed up any further at home. I finally got to the magic number of five minutes apart right at midnight. My parents and I packed up and headed to the hospital.

I was admitted and wheeled up to the Mother/Baby floor where they performed a "check" that no one warned me about. The nurse inserted her entire hand into my vagina during a contraction to make sure my cervix was actually dilating more during contractions. This was the only time I yelled out a swear word during the whole process. It was an intense pinching pain and I looked my mom in the eyes and said, "You are fucking insane to have more than one kid." Once the nurse confirmed that yes, I was dilating more with each contraction, they admitted me to a delivery room. It was at this point that several things happened at once. I began throwing up uncontrollably and the nurses looked at my puke and said, "Oooh! Pizza! What kind?"

I asked my dad to start calling the people on the list who wanted to be at the hospital. He obliged, and then I was told to continue walking around to help my cervix dilate. I tried my best to walk around but kept having to stop to breathe through contractions and throw up. When I got to a "five" they had me lay down so I could get anti-nausea medicine through my IV and get my epidural. By the time both of those kicked in it was 4:00am. Parker and his parents arrived right around then, even though my dad had called them around 1:30am and they had insisted they would be down right away. When Parker walked into the room I could smell alcohol and smoke and immediately knew he had been at a party. It was a Saturday night, after all. I asked him why in the world he had gone to a party when he knew I was past my due date and he got very offended and paced back and forth for awhile, but kept his mouth in check since both of my parents were still in the room. A little after 4:00, when my emotions settled down and my medications were working, I actually dozed into a light sleep. My dad gave me my pillow and teddy bear and excused himself to the waiting room, where remained to greet my friends as they started showing up to wait for the birth. My mom pulled up a chair on my right side and dozed next to me, but was stroking my arm off and on the whole time. Mr. Narcissist, however, couldn't handle that things were happening slowly, and stomped off to the waiting room to sleep off some of the drugs and alcohol he had consumed mere hours ago. For four glorious hours, it was just me and my mom in the room, dozing and peacefully keeping an eye on my contractions as they slowly progressed.

I woke up with a start at 8:15am and announced that it was time to push. My mom went to find a nurse and soon I was being checked and monitored very closely. I started pushing around 8:30am and the next two hours are intermittently blocked from my memory. I know that at some point my ex-boyfriend reentered the room and held my left leg while my mom held my right. I know that there were residents and student nurses doing clinicals that popped in and out of the room randomly. I know that I was starving but all I could eat were ice chips. At 10:30am, my epidural started to wear off and each push brought a sharper pain. The contractions were happening rapidly and it was harder to catch my breath in between. The midwife kept telling me I was almost there, but it was hard to believe her because she was saying it after every push. At the very end, there were three big pushes and I suddenly understood what one of my aunts meant when she described "the ring of fire," as my daughter made her entry into the world at 10:58am on Sunday, March 15, 2009. As soon as she left me, I began sobbing uncontrollably and my mom held me tight. When she released me I looked to my left to see what Parker had to say for himself, but he was gone. I propped up on my elbows and found him with the nurses who were cleaning off the baby and running tests. Once they finished, they handed her to him and he got to hold her for a full two minutes before they told him to bring her to me. I spent those two minutes pushing out the afterbirth and being super pissed. For one thing, I didn't realize I would still be having painful contractions after the baby was out. For another thing, why the hell was this asshole holding my baby and acting like he contributed anything to her growth and development over the last nine months? When he brought her to me, I held her tight for a few brief moments and he filled me in that she weighed nine pounds and three ounces and was nineteen and a half inches long. I got even more pissed that the nurses had told him that information before they told me. And then, just like that, she was whisked away from me by the nurses because she and I both had a fever and they wanted to monitor both of us.

The days that followed her birth led me into a state of depression and rage I had never known before. There were things happening to my body that no one had warned me about: I was still bleeding, I felt as though I had just gotten hit by a truck, my belly was jiggly and wrinkly, and I had to use a squirt bottle when I peed instead of wiping. I could barely stay awake in the hospital, but I was awake enough to know that Parker and both of his parents were flitting about as if they had just won the lottery. They were inviting family members that I had never met to come and gawk at me and my daughter. They were treating her like a trophy and completely ignoring me and all the work I had done to get her here. They insisted that he would spend the night in the hospital with me because he was so in love with his new baby and just wanted to be there for her. He didn't realize I was going to need just as much care as the baby throughout the night and got verbally abusive with me several times during my hospital stay. The worst time was when I was trying to breastfeed but she wouldn't latch and she kept crying, which woke him up. He was upset that I was letting her cry this much and that he couldn't sleep. I tried to explain that for some reason she was having trouble latching, and I ended up crying because I was at a complete loss for how to help her. He then tried to shove a pacifier in her mouth and she was whipping her head back and forth to push it back out. She made some grunts and coughing noises and I was terrified that she was choking. I asked him to stop in case she was choking and then he turned on me and started screaming that I was a bitch for accusing him of trying to choke his baby. He must have gotten pretty loud because within several minutes there were three nurses and a doctor in the room. I was a crying mess, Jocelyn was still wailing for food, and he was standing over both of us with hate in his eyes. They were able to get him to calm down and offered to let him go sleep in the waiting room while they helped me. He did so, and exited the room for the rest of the night. I couldn't stop crying and the nurse proceeded to ask me several questions that I'm sure she was required to ask by DCFS as a mandated reporter. Fortunately, I was able to say that no, I was not living with him. No, he had never gotten physical with me, he just really liked to scream at me. Yes, I felt safe in my residence and no, he had never made threats against me.

I brought my chubby-cheeked girl home on St. Patrick's Day. When we arrived home, I collapsed on the couch and slept for a few hours while my parents took care of her. When I woke up from that nap, I asked them if I would ever get to sleep through the night again. They both chuckled and said, "Yes, but it will be awhile. We're here to help you through the days so that you can get through the nights on your own." That was the basis of our relationship for the rest of the time I lived there: they helped as much or as little as I needed them to during the day, but the nights were my responsibility. It was a solid system that worked well for us as a family. It was not always sunshine, rainbows, and unicorns, but it was a stable and structured means to cope with the new stress and routines in the house.

I returned to classes when Jocelyn was nine days old. I had given birth on the Sunday of my spring break, and I returned to school the following Tuesday. I returned to work in mid-April when she was one month old. I felt like a zombie wandering through a sea of perky college kids, but the positive side was that when I was at work or school I could just be myself, not a teenage mom. I finished my year at my junior college and transferred to Bradley University that fall, as I had planned. I had no idea that when I showed up to a meeting with Dr. Nina Collins, my guidance counselor at Bradley, that I was meeting an angel on earth. I explained my situation to her and that I would like to graduate as quickly as possible so that I could start working to support my daughter on my own. She listened intently and then scribbled on her notepad furiously for several minutes. Then she proudly turned it around and showed me a detailed semester-by-semester plan with a graduation date of December, 2011. She said, "This is the earliest I can get you your degree, and it will be a mad dash, but I know you can do it." It was indeed a mad dash, and that was the first of many times Dr. Collins made a positive impact on my life. Because of her, I graduated in December of 2011 with a Bachelor of Science in Family & Consumer Sciences: Teacher Education, and was told, by the President of Bradley University as I walked across the stage, that my story was an inspiration.

November, 2018

Now I am a 30-year old with a ten-year-old daughter. I still think of that night in the Schnuck's bathroom when I saw two pink lines as a defining moment in my life. But I have learned that it was not my only defining moment. In the Fall of 2011, I met a guy named Kevin. In 2012, Kevin asked me on a date and we immediately clicked. When we became an "official" couple, Parker called to let me know that he was genuinely happy for me, and that he knew Kevin from a long time ago and thought that he was a great guy. Later that year, Parker enrolled himself in a rehabilitation center in South Florida, and when he graduated from the program he decided to stay there. In 2013, Kevin proposed and we moved into a tiny apartment in Peoria with Jocelyn. She started calling him, "dad," in that apartment, and we planned our wedding and our future there. In 2014, we bought our first house, and when we got married, Jocelyn was our flower girl. In 2015, Kevin called Parker to ask his thoughts on adopting Jocelyn. Since Parker had only seen Jocelyn once and had spoken to her on the phone a handful of times since he left in 2012, he quickly agreed that the adoption was a great idea. Kevin legally adopted her in April of that year and she chose to change her name to his. She started begging us for younger siblings as soon as we got married, and we tried to appease her by adopting two cats and two dogs.

In 2018, we decided we were ready to give Jocelyn a human sibling. I am currently expecting a baby boy. With due dates only two months apart, there are many ways that I feel like I am reliving my pregnancy with Jocelyn, a decade later. I spent the summer being sweaty, tired, and nauseous, only this time there was no vomiting. Telling everyone I was pregnant was a recurring celebration rather than a "situation." I spent the fall eating all of the food that was in front of me and this time I kept down all of the prenatal vitamins. The second trimester was surprisingly fun and I enjoyed every minute of it. We did not do a Gender Reveal party, but we did buy a special "gender" balloon for Jocelyn to pop as a surprise. This time I knew I needed to include my husband and daughter in deciding a name for the baby. Together we came up with Kendrick Mason, Kenny for short. I'm currently in my third trimester and am quite uncomfortably large. I am a high school Foods teacher who still climbs three flights of stairs to my classroom every day and is prepping sub plans for my twelve-week maternity leave. I am gearing up for my last holiday season as a mother of one, which is a bittersweet feeling. Jocelyn is in fourth grade, gets straight A's, and is on a competitive dance team. She is spunky, headstrong, kind, and unique. She still only talks to Parker on the phone several times a year, and he has since moved from Florida to New York and then on to New Jersey. He flies back to visit home once a year and usually makes time to visit with her one of the days he's here. Parker's parents have not seen or spoken to Jocelyn since 2011, and he is on board with that decision.

Even though everything about this pregnancy fits the "normal" mold that I so desperately craved when I was carrying Jocelyn, I still battle anxiety and negative thoughts about myself on a daily basis. I am a recovering perfectionist who continues to learn how to let go of meaningless worries, and I have to remind myself often that there is no such thing as a perfect mother or a perfect family. Kevin is wonderful and has accepted his role as a father with full devotion, but he is not a perfect person either. We continue to work out the kinks of our family dynamic with Jocelyn, and I anticipate that the new baby will change that dynamic further. Kevin is a full-time employee of the Army National Guard and is mandated to attend two different two-week training sessions out-of-state after the baby is born. When he first told me about both sessions, I got very quiet and tears welled. I was silently reliving all those nights spent alone with Jocelyn and how difficult they had been. He didn't understand that his news was bringing up those feelings of abandonment from so long ago, but once I explained, he felt horrible. Seeing his empathy and compassion made all the difference. I was reminded that although I will be alone with a baby for an extended period of time, the circumstances are completely different this time. I have a partner who plans to contribute as equally as he can, and who takes his role as one of our family's providers seriously.

My life still has plenty of opportunities for Big Moments where everything could change and I look forward to those days. Watching Jocelyn grow up has shown me how rewarding it is to help her through her own Big Moments. Nothing has taught me that life is bigger than myself quite like motherhood. Even though the days are exhausting, the years have passed quickly and she continues to be my greatest accomplishment.

A Surrogate Mother

By Devin Boles

In 2009, I decided to be a surrogate mother. My husband's niece told me about her surrogacy journey and I fell in love with the idea. I loved both of my pregnancies and would have had more children. My husband and I already had two children each from previous relationships, and he had a vasectomy years before we met. But I still wanted us to experience a pregnancy together. And I wanted to give another woman the gift of being a mother.

As soon as my husband supported my intention, I started researching the process.

We contacted Reproductive Possibilities in New Jersey in the summer of 2009. This was the same agency that my husband's niece successfully used. There was a lengthy application process and we had to list our interests, beliefs, intentions, as well as our family dynamics. We had to divulge our entire life story, and though it was quite invasive, we felt it justifiable for the cause. After our application was reviewed and accepted, Reproductive Possibilities then created our very detailed profile so potential parents could view every aspect of our lives.

We were told it might be weeks or months before potential parents would select us. We weren't even sure if we'd ever be selected. But just a few months later, in November 2009, we got the call that a couple had selected us for a phone interview. The phone call would be with the potential parents, an agent from RP, my husband, and me. The potential parents asked a lot of questions and told us their story. They already had one son, a toddler, and wanted him to have a sibling. The woman had developed a lung disease and wasn't able to safely carry anymore children. They said that they were wanting to use their own egg and sperm to create the embryo, later implanting it into a surrogate. This is called being a gestational carrier. I would "only" be carrying their child, with none of my own DNA. The four of us instantly connected. The potential parents sounded wonderful and I truly wanted to help them.

After we got the phone call that the potential parents chose us, we also had to decide if we wanted to move forward or not. There were intense decisions to make. This wasn't simply a matter of deciding whether I wanted to carry a baby for another couple. I needed to decide how many embryos I would allow to be implanted, if I would carry multiple children in the event that it should happen, and would I be able to terminate the pregnancy if there were health risks involved for me or the baby. The biggest issue would be carrying and delivering a baby, somebody else's baby, and then handing it over to them.

I could do this and I wanted to do this.

My husband and I were both so excited, and the answers to all of the decisions were easy. Of course I would do this for these people. The woman and I exchanged email addresses and phone numbers. We could then communicate without going through RP. She said we would also keep in contact through the years so I could watch the child or children grow. The kid(s) would know that they grew in another woman's belly, and though I would not be able to raise them, I would be able to see them through the years. I felt this was a great relationship, I felt positive about the process, and I felt like we would both find happiness in this endeavor.

RP set us up with an attorney from Chicago. The intended parents had their own. Paperwork was drawn up protecting my rights and my body. Their paperwork protected their embryo and their child or children after they were born. I wasn't scared or nervous about any of it. I knew it would be their baby and I didn't feel I'd have any post-delivery issues with letting go. The intended parents would pay for all the medical and travel expenses. We wouldn't pay for anything out of pocket. There would also be compensation paid to me after the birth. Many people wondered and asked me about this amount and some suggested I was only doing this for the money. This was offensive because I was doing this to experience another pregnancy, to bring life into the world, and to help someone else who genuinely needed it. The money was inconsequential.

The intended parents flew me and my husband out to Penn Fertility Clinic after we had everything signed with the lawyers. They lived in Philadelphia and one of the best fertility clinics in the U.S. happened to be in Philadelphia. I was examined by a fertility physician, they explained how the process would work, and then my husband and I had to undergo a psychiatric evaluation.

Everything went perfectly and I was another step closer in this journey. I was allowed to go home and we would travel back to Penn Clinic for the embryo transfer in a few months.

When I first heard the term "progesterone shots," I wasn't nervous or worried. I was only excited to start the process. The physician explained that the shot was intramuscular and I'd have to get it in my hip each day. We decided that my sister, a nurse, would be the one to start giving me my shots. She came by my work every morning, we'd go into the small bathroom together, and she'd stick me. These shots continued for six long weeks as they were preparing my body for pregnancy and preventing potential rejection of the embryos.

These shots. My emotions. This was real. I was extremely hormonal and I cried constantly.

The progesterone needle was huge and very painful, and each day, the pain increased. My hips were bruised and sore and the thought of each shot brought tears to my eyes; I was anxious over each stick.

After successfully completing the hormone shot regimen, it was finally time for us to travel to Pennsylvania for the embryo transfer. The big day was scheduled for May 14th.

We were in a period of really bad weather. The airport was delaying and canceling flights. My body was ready for this transfer and we had to get to Philly. Knowing what I had just invested in this process and that the timing was imperative due to the hormone shot schedule, we absolutely had to fly immediately. In desperation, my sister drove us to Chicago so we could catch the quickest flight. We made it on schedule, but barely.

The biological parents booked us an amazing hotel room in downtown Philadelphia. The intended mother brought me beautiful yellow roses. They invited us over to their house so we could see where they lived and meet their son. They made us feel so welcome and we loved our visit. We had a barbecue with them and were excited to bring another member to their family.

The next day was the transfer. I was a little nervous but mostly excited. They had two embryos to transfer, and the doctor said the transfer wouldn't hurt and would only feel like a pelvic exam.

It was quick. They did a sonogram of my uterus and the doctor watched as she carefully placed the embryos inside. After mere minutes, it was done, and I was so hopeful for this family.

My husband and I went back to the hotel and for the next twelve hours, I laid in bed to rest.

After my twelve-hour required calm, we had one more day before we flew back home. My husband and I decided to drive into New York City to see the Statue of Liberty. It was a quick trip, but we had a good day.

We flew back home feeling nervous but certain that everything was good.

The subsequent waiting, however, was the worst. I wasn't supposed to take a home pregnancy test because it wouldn't be accurate due to the injected hormones. But I felt pregnant. I knew it was going to work. My mother's intuition was already strong.

A couple of weeks later, I was scheduled for blood work at my local hospital where we would learn if the embryo transfer was successful. I had no doubts that it was. I was excited for the genetic parents and for us and for the baby, and I couldn't wait to use my body for such a good cause.

Two hours later, I got a phone call from the hospital. It wasn't the call that I expected.

I was not pregnant. Neither embryo attached.

I couldn't see. I couldn't talk. I couldn't breathe. I was devastated.

These were not embryos to me. They were babies. These were lives. And not only did I have this great feeling of loss for myself, I felt like I had let the biological parents down. They were counting on me and this was their only chance to have a bigger family. I was their healthy body, their healthy uterus, and I couldn't understand why neither embryo attached. I was fixated on the idea that maybe they did attach, if even for a small period of time, and then something happened. Was I pregnant and then not pregnant? The fertility doctor said that we had great odds. Even greater with using two embryos. I did everything I was supposed to do. The treatments, the traveling, the resting. I had already had two pregnancies with no complications. My body should have known how to do this. It didn't. It failed me, and I failed the parents whom I had come to love, and I failed this baby who could have been.

I felt very alone. And I felt so sad.

Nobody could understand my pain and guilt. I didn't even feel like my husband understood. Of course everyone was supportive and sad. They said things like, "It wasn't meant to be. God had other plans," or "It wasn't your fault." But these words only upset me more. I felt in my bones that this was meant to be. I was supposed to do this; I was made to do this. I wanted this more than anything else. This failure was, with certainty, my fault.

My heart broke. I wasn't able to help the intended parents like I had thought. This poor mother was my friend now and I was the reason she couldn't have the family she wanted.

After we had the terrible job of telling everyone that the embryos did not survive, the biological mother went through a time of grief. She later reached out to me and told me I wasn't to blame and there was nothing we could have done differently. She and her husband also decided not to try again. Though I wanted them to be able to expand their family, I didn't think I could have endured the whole process another time had they asked me. Especially if it didn't work again.

RP had told me that when I was ready, they would put our profile back up for review. But I couldn't bear another heartbreak. As much as I wanted to do this initially, after the embryo transfer had failed, I couldn't put myself, my family, or another hopeful family through this again.

Even after a decade, I still get sad when I think about this journey. It was long ago and I don't talk about it much anymore.

But I do think about it and I wonder how things could have been different. I wonder why it didn't work for us. With each passing year, I imagine how old "they" would be and what they might be doing had they survived. I also think about the intended mother. We haven't talked in many years, but when I do think of her, I relive her sadness and wonder how often she thinks of our journey, too.

But overall, when I reflect on my surrogacy journey, I just wish I could have done this for her and her family and for those two babies.

Year 7 A.B.[1]

By Sarah Kazarian

When we have multiple children, we create them, see them, and raise them through different lenses. Each child is brought into a completely new family dynamic. I wish I could look at each child with the same eyes and hold the same expectations. But it's simply not possible.

I cannot remember what happened before the end of August, 2010, but I do know it took my husband, Dave, and I a few months to conceive Ava. I knew it was her when I saw the double lines. But those months trying were agonizing. Dave kept reassuring me that, kids or no kids, we would have a happy life together. He's pretty great like that. But we finally did it. And I felt accomplished. Like this was what I was meant to be doing: growing babies. I didn't get sick. My blood pressure was perfect, and I only gained seventy pounds (sarcasm: not recommended). She was worth it.

Before having kids, I participated in many unhealthy habits. I ate the wrong foods (sometimes out of the garbage), drank the strong drinks (can't even tell you what out of), smoked the

---

1. After Babies

good stuff. I had fun. I lived life hard, and rarely turned down a dare or an adventure, so much so that people from my past are generally surprised that I now have four kids and two dogs. But I'm not surprised. I always binge life. Burn the candle at both ends. It's who I am.

Pregnancy with Ava was easy, and finding out she was a girl was amazing. But during our second ultrasound, we were given some pretty heavy information. The tech found a "calcium deposit" in one of her heart valves. This was terrifying, and I had no idea what it implied. A doctor informed us that it was an indicator of Down Syndrome. Scary, but as a special educator, I knew what that entailed. Or at least I thought I did. And Dave would tell me that if she had special needs, how perfect that I was her mother. I still grieved the pregnancy and carried a cloud with me until she was born. It was hard for me to connect. I was afraid. I should have talked to someone. Who wants to spend twenty weeks depressed over an uncontrollable "what if?"

I chose an OB practice that had a great reputation. It was a group of six doctors and I liked most of them. They gave me laid-back advice and we had fun. I thought it was perfect.

I wasn't really educated on how women could have babies, and I only blame myself for that. I should have sought out information from other women that I trusted. I didn't though, and just followed the path that was before me. I went for my check-ups, and when we got closer to the end they talked about induction and I listened. Thankfully, it was unnecessary. On Thursday, June 2, 2011, five days before her due date, I started getting contractions. I vacuumed the house and the contractions increased. We had Mexican food for dinner. I freaked. I tried to sleep but couldn't and ended up going into the hospital after laboring for two hours at home. It was too soon, but I was scared. And I trusted that my group would take care of me with the highest respect for me, my body, and my baby.

After laboring for a long time, I got an epidural (I wanted one) and I couldn't feel my legs. At all. I got some rest. They decided I needed to have my water broken to help things move along (I mean, I was just laying there, so how were things supposed to progress…). I kept getting checked and they told me when I was getting ready to push. They held my legs, I pushed for twenty minutes, and then the doctor in charge (from my trusted group) decided I needed an episiotomy to move things along a little quicker. That worked and my beautiful, tiny baby girl was born. No special needs. 9/9 Apgar. Gorgeous. She still is, but I wish I had given her a more natural introduction into this world.

Ava never slept. But that's how I thought all babies were. I never questioned the every-two-hours nursing sessions, but I was thankful for my wild, sleepless twenties that helped me to prepare for this time. I functioned. It wasn't fun, but I was able to function. In yoga pants, I finished my master's degree during Ava's first year earthside with the help of my mom and my sister. She was my little sidekick and came with me everywhere. I liked being her mom so much that I ended up never going back to work after she was born. This was the best decision I could have made for myself, but even good decisions have consequences.

Staying home and raising children has been an identity-losing, brian-numbing, humbling, awesome, exhausting experience. One for which I am thankful. Which is ironic. However, one emotion I wasn't prepared to have to endure was guilt. Guilt over everything. Guilt over not giving her the experience of other children in a childcare setting, guilt of her birth, guilt of not spending enough time with her because I made her a big sister too soon.

The moment came when I was washing dishes late in March 2012. Ava was nine months old, and I could smell the dirt in the planted pots on the windowsill. Then the dogs started intensifying their annoying behaviors, and then I got my telltale sign. I got a ligament cramp when I tried to get out of bed. I knew it before the double lines showed up. How was I going to tell Dave we were having another baby? I was worried about him not being ready (I had no choice but to be ready, of course), but he took it surprisingly well. And there we had it. A little sister. Little Drea Grayce, our surprise, growing inside me.

This little baby also gave us a scare during ultrasounds. Her little heart would stop beating for what felt like hours, but actually seconds, and then would start up again. She ended up growing out of it, but after that, no more ultrasounds for me. I was determined to stick to the limited intervention plan for baby number two.

I learned a lot after Ava's birth and gained a new friend, terrible migraines. So, with Drea's birth, I decided to eschew all medical interventions. By this time in my life, my habits had completely shifted and I went from eating food from the corner gas station to eating an organic, BPA free, grass-fed, non-GMO, naturally colorful diet. And I had friends who believed in the same crunchy ways, so finding resources this time around was easy. I self-studied birthing practices through Hypnobabies, I found a single birth practitioner who believed I could do it, I taught Dave how to be my doula, and I was ready to labor this time.

Well, nothing ever goes to plan, and this little girl decided to come late and I had no patience, so at five centimeters dilated, and 50% effaced, I decided to get my membranes swept. My doctor insisted that I be checked into labor and delivery immediately following my appointment. It was so surreal, checking into L&D without contractions. Even the nurses were like, "really?" Dave and I knew better this time, so we walked the halls for hours until contractions started and intensified. I jammed out to some inappropriate gangster rap, and this little nugget came out four and a half hours after the first contraction (to some pretty inappropriate rap music). We really lucked out. She had meconium in her fluids, but was completely healthy. Amazing. She was incredible. Strong. Beautiful. She was born resilient and I was ready to go home a few hours later, but had to stay two nights in the hospital. However, I was sold on a non-medicated childbirth.

Nursing Drea was another story. Nursing Ava had been annoying and constant, but easy. I started drying up when I got pregnant, but we made it to a year and it was never very painful. Drea's latch was strong and shallow. Bad combo. I had cracks and blood coming from my nipples by the end of the third day. I remember sobbing in bed, scared to feed my baby. Stupidly, I never called a lactation consultant. But, I did push through and thankfully we figured it out. By the second week, the pain was gone and we were nursing strong.

To conceive our third, Dave and I used the Shettles method. It was recommended to us by a neighbor as a way to pick the sex of your baby. It worked, and along came Oscar. The pregnancy was easy and I only gained fifty pounds. His labor (which I expected to be similar to Drea's) was horrendous. Long and painful. I can't even remember the music I used to motivate me during labor. I remember the top of the bed, as I rocked on all fours for (what felt like) days. His umbilical cord was wrapped around his neck, my only clue as to why that labor was so intense.

Being able to grow a baby feels powerful. Superhuman. Birthing a baby feels the same, even when the labor is long and intensive. Oscar, thankfully, was easy once he came out. He was actually my easiest child until he learned how to crawl out of his crib (at about twenty months). He nursed well and slept (on his belly...) well. Three kids in three years.

After three kids, it became hard to decipher which memory was for which kid. More mom guilt. It is now hard to even remember a time when I only had three kids. I know it was hard. Stressful. I had no time for one kid, just fleeting moments with each. Guilt for having the big two watch television while I nursed the third, guilt for being frustrated and stressed, guilt for not being able to be "there" when someone needed me. It was hard for me to walk the dog because I didn't have a triple stroller. Life changed with three. It was the hardest thing I had ever done. Balancing time and hugs was impossible. Especially in the beginning. I refused to have another baby after Oscar. And then came Lucy.

Again, pregnancy was easy (I only gained thirty-five pounds with her), but her labor was lonely. Dave, being bored after the first three births, slept on the couch while the lone nurse and I went through the motions, both of us occasionally giving him death stares. I labored very internally and this time there was not much for him to do, but I still wish he would have been awake, standing beside me. Lucy had a hard time turning past my tailbone and she bruised it pretty badly. Her labor was awesome until the last hour. (My tailbone still hurts if I think about it.) But some Zydeco and Bob Marley helped me through her labor and she finally came out. Hers was my most emotional birth. My last baby, and I knew it. Clouded with bittersweet feelings.

Growing a child in your body is surreal. Almost alien. But I love it. Crave it. I miss it. But the life that is left in its path of parenthood is primal. It's do or die. That feeling has intensified over the years as our brood has grown, but I think it is at the core of all parenting. There are so many things to remember and constantly worry about, which makes mom-life exhausting. But we become strong enough to digest it all. More often than not, all I can see is the complaining, chores, meals, homework, chores, pets, bills, chores, and chores. And the guilt. But then I slow down occasionally and enjoy the amazing thing that is happening. I'll recognize the to do list, and then do something not on it to remind myself of what is important.

Parenthood is defined by the immeasurable work we do. How do you make sure you're doing everything right? You can't. Parenting is like a twenty-year assignment for which you have no rubric, and the teacher is unreachable. I'm not even sure there is a test at the end. You just sort of do your best, love your kids, and hope. That's it. Seems so simple and so vague. Yet it is the hardest thing I've ever done in my life. Is there constant guilt and question over every. single. choice? Yes. Would I do it again? Of course, without hesitation. But ask me again during the teenage years. My lenses might be pretty cloudy and cracked by then.

Dismissed

By Casey Pfeifer

We were all wasted on a lake, sitting on top of a giant floating mat when my friend tearfully apologized to me for downplaying my feelings about a C-section. Drunk words are sober thoughts, so she finally had the liquid courage to tell me that she blew off my concern when my doctor put a bug in my ear that I may have to have a C-section with my first child. She said until her sister-in-law had a C-section and explained her feelings, my friend disregarded mine, but now with new empathy, she told me over and over how inconsiderate that was. While I was grateful for her change of heart, this is what is frustrating about motherhood: people think that because they had a mom, or couldn't be a mom, or are a mom, that they are entitled to tell you how to feel as a mom or how to handle your mom game. Everyone is quick to squelch your birthing fears with, "Girl, birthing is the easy part." That was not my experience.

Of all the birthing nightmares that kept me awake in my early twenties, none of these would compare to the fear I felt when my doctor said I may have to have a C-section due to my narrow hips. I was thirty years old and thirty-five weeks pregnant. By the end of the pregnancy, my baby was a week overdue, so I talked incessantly about having to get "carved up" to get him out. My nightmares had resurfaced, but this time, pushing a baby out of my vagina didn't seem so bad when compared to the alternative.

Lying awake in my early twenties thinking that I could not push out a baby was like a prophecy. Before I had my son, I specifically remember comparing hip width to girls who had already pushed a kid out; I had serious doubts. In the end, I was right. What is interesting, or maybe more frustrating, is that the more educated I became on the two types of birth, it was not lost on me that a "natural" birth was no longer used to describe birthing with no drugs, but was used to describe a vaginal birth. Already, a woman is marked as "unnatural" if a baby doesn't exit through a vagina. In fact, the vaginal birth as "natural" is cloaked in downplaying a woman's fears by implying the antiquated narrative that a woman should just be grateful to have a healthy baby. That, as long as the baby safely arrives into the world, it doesn't matter how. I knew people fed this to women, but I thought my friends would be more enlightened and sympathetic. And when I turned to them to express my concerns, I found that to alleviate my fears, they had to first invalidate my feelings. "Carved up? You're not a turkey, Casey. You will have a healthy kid, and it doesn't matter how they come into this world." But it does. Or at least it does to me.

When my doctor told me I may end up on the operating table, I called my best friend, who was the most sympathetic. She told me about her C-section plan that she put in place in case her birth story ended in the operating room. She also reminded me that I was in the hands of one of the most capable hospitals, if not the most capable, in the state. My mom repeated, "You don't know that you have to get one until you go into labor. Try not to worry." I was a woman possessed. All I did was talk about the weight of the baby. I convinced myself that I was going to deliver early because the doctor and sonographer were a week off on my due date. I went a week late instead. One of my students (I am a high school teacher) had Tarot cards for sport and predicted I would go six days early. I have never been to a psychic in my life, but when he laid out those cards and proclaimed January 24th as my projected due date, I took it as gospel. I wanted a vaginal delivery so badly that it made me ache. But when I told my friends this, so many only glossed over my feelings with positive C-section stories and the idea that my baby coming out healthy was what was most important. I left those conversations feeling selfish and cowardly to the point where I didn't question my own gut instincts because I was embarrassed at the way I was feeling. After all, there are some women who would feel lucky to be in my situation, and I understood that. But being lucky doesn't make going through a major surgery any less intimidating.

.   .   .

I went into labor naturally on the morning I was to be induced. I had dull pain at around 1:30am and had contractions five to seven minutes apart at around 3:00am. I basically got no sleep the night before I went into labor. I stopped dilating at five centimeters, and my son's heartbeat decreased significantly when my doctor ordered pitocin. The resident told me at 8:00pm, after laboring for roughly sixteen hours, that my baby was not responding well to labor. I knew it was time to throw in the towel. The decreased heart rate was concerning. I accepted the fact that I would have been one of those women in the 1800s who died in childbirth. Tears welled up in my eyes as I agreed with her that a

C-section was probably necessary. I was exhausted by that point and was ready to deliver a throat punch to the next person that dug their fingers into my cervix. The anesthesiologist had me take a shot of medication that would neutralize my stomach for surgery so I wouldn't get sick. The baby-faced resident asked if I would accept blood for a transfusion, but made me aware of my odds of getting HIV. She assured me, however, that she had never seen it happen in her career. A fucking resident. I don't remember the figure, but she posed it as one person at a Taylor Swift concert getting HIV. I wanted to tell her that I knew three people who had attended a T. Swift concert, so that was kind of a fucked up way of presenting those odds.

My husband, Ryan, couldn't be in the operating room while it was being prepped. A room full of people surrounded me and stared at me as they stated their names. My arms were splayed like Jesus on the cross, so as they methodically stated their names, I felt like I was about to be a sacrifice for their cult gathering. I will say, I don't know if it was the drugs or the nice people in the room, but the operating room was the most peace I had had in hours. I was finally at the end. I was ready to hear my baby cry. The doctors warned me about feeling like someone was sitting on my chest when they pushed my kid out for me. All of it sounds so gruesome now, but it truly was a few minutes of relief. I had labored for so long, so it seemed like a miracle that they could guarantee I would see my kid in less than a half hour.

Reality set in when I had to be in a post operating room for an entire hour. Luckily, Ryan came and sat with me, but it was just us in an incredibly cold room while everyone else got to be with my baby. This killed me. When my son, Simon, was briefly placed on the table for me to look at him immediately after birth, I teared up out of joy. They swiftly took him away while the surgery came to a close, and it felt like they ripped him away from me. When given a C-section, mother and baby are not allowed to have this time because both are prone to infection. Or at least that is the impression I got from them. No one explained things to me that well and I just wanted to be with my son.

My recovery was hellish. My incision didn't drain so it had to be drained manually. My abdomen was so sore that laying my baby on top of my stomach to breastfeed was intensely painful. I broke out in hives from the painkillers, so I eventually had to live without them. I could hardly move for over two weeks. I consider myself a mentally strong person, but I was constantly having to separate how I was feeling about my new family, which was overjoyed, and how I felt physically, which was fucking terrible. If I laid down, I was in pain. If I sat up in a chair, I was in pain. If I stood, I was in pain. Women claiming they forget the pains of childbirth are full of shit. You remember, you just decide a baby is worth a second birth.

There are no absolutes when it comes to childbirth or how each woman will feel about it. I am still somewhat flabbergasted thinking about the scoffs and dismissals I heard when I would tell others about my fear of having to undergo a major surgery in order to meet my baby. One of my most emotional moments regarding how I felt about the birth of my first kid flooded back that day at the lake when my friend, who has shown me limitless compassion and no judgment throughout our entire friendship, apologized for the time she dismissed my fears and feelings. Floating on a mat while day drinking was the first time I allowed myself to admit that people had dismissed me. It was the first time I didn't feel selfish for hating that I had to have a C-section. Our slurred apologies and acceptances were exactly what helped me overcome the small jabs I took as I expressed my fears leading up to having my son. And since I plan on having another child, and subsequently, another C-section, I will walk into my next scheduled birth feeling all of the feelings that I feel, and I will bitch about it as much as I please. And I will not feel shame about it this time.

Goji Berries and Lamb Chops

By Amanda Berkes

Since I was a little girl, I knew I would be a mother. I'd make believe I had four kids, two boys and two girls, and I'd come up with names for my future children. I was always a mother hen to my three younger siblings. As a teenager, I spent a lot of time with my younger cousins, driving them to sporting events, getting them ready for school, even participating in parent-tot swim lessons. These were things I was good at, and these were things I loved doing. I was born a mother.

After I nearly failed my first chemistry class in college, I realized my science-heavy major wasn't for me. I headed to the career center to research new options and I narrowed my search based on jobs that would be best for a working mom. As a twenty-year-old, I chose to be a teacher because I wouldn't have to travel, my schedule would be predictable, and I'd have lengthy breaks to spend with my kids. I chose my future, my career, based around the fact that I would have kids.

When I was twenty-one and coming home from my late night shift at a shitty college bar, I randomly met a guy hanging out on the stairs of my apartment building. We ended up talking for hours, mostly about things I can no longer remember, but when he told me, "we're going to get married and have four kids one day," my heart fluttered. I had met my husband.

While we were dating, I finished two master's degrees. After all, it made sense to complete my education before kids came along. After we got married, we bought a four-bedroom house with a big backyard, figuring our kids would love sledding down the massive hill. When I purchased my first new car, I made sure it had highly rated backseat safety scores because I wanted only the best for my future babies. When we got married, we splurged on a honeymoon to Europe because we knew our days of child-free travel were limited. Soon after our wedding, my husband decided to get an MBA. I counted out the classes he would have to take and suggested he double up his load each semester and take summer classes so he could finish his degree before we decided to start a family. Although it nearly killed him, he agreed to the rigorous schedule and he was set to finish in record time. When my childhood friend asked me to stand up for her wedding, I told her my plans to get pregnant and I ordered a dress three sizes larger.

We had planned everything out perfectly. Now, all I had to do was stop taking birth control.

No luck during the first month. But who gets pregnant on their first try anyway?

It didn't happen the second month either. I wasn't too worried, but I bought ovulation tests to help. Then, I purchased a fancier ovulation kit. Still nothing. Month after month, there was only disappointment and frustration. Maybe a fertility calendar? No, only more negative results. And more crying. In desperation, I completely changed my diet, and although it made me cranky, it didn't make me pregnant.

My husband's graduation arrived. There was no baby, and I wasn't even pregnant. Why did I force him to finish so quickly? My friend's wedding came and I wasn't pregnant for that either. I was stuck with that too-big frumpy dress that made me look fat, even though I was losing weight from stress. Trying to conceive consumed my life. When I went out to dinner with my friend soon after her honeymoon, she told me she was pregnant. I was happy for her, but so sorry for myself. Later that night, I cried myself to sleep.

Something wasn't right. How could this not be working? I met with a naturopathic doctor, hoping he would solve the mystery. I did tests and ultrasounds, but it turned out I was fairly normal. However, he suggested that my husband do a semen analysis.

Of course, my husband agreed to do the test right away, not knowing it would be a traumatic feat of concentration, having to provide a sample in a public restroom with constant knocking on the door.

The results came back while he was playing golf and I was at my parent's eating dinner. He texted me the news—he had zero sperm. Is that even possible? I couldn't get upset in front of my family; they had no idea what we were going through, so my genuine reaction would have to wait. I hurried through dinner, and on my drive home I screamed so loud I scared myself. At home I nearly threw up. This was bad. I hugged my husband and he apologized, even though none of this was his fault. He told me he loved me but he wouldn't blame me for finding another man who could give me children.

And that's how we lived for a while. Heartbroken and depressed, our thoughts taking us to dark places. More tests confirmed the same thing, no sperm, no chance for a baby. It was so confusing. We were responsible, we had planned for this. I thought we'd be great parents. Why was I getting punished? Would I not make a good mother?

Everyday life became hard with this weight constantly pulling me down. I'd pull into the garage but found I didn't have the energy to actually get out of the car, so I'd sit silently in the dark. I'd go to bed lucky I could forget our predicament for the night, and each morning I'd wake up and enjoy one second of forgetfulness before my stomach dropped and I remembered our reality. People at work were starting to ask if everything was all right because my eyes were sometimes still puffy from crying. I avoided social situations because the conversation somehow migrated to the topic of children, and someone would always ask when I was going to start a family. How can you politely tell your grandma to mind her business? When I was invited to a baptism, I opted to skip it last minute, not thinking I could handle seeing cheerful people with a newborn. And when the baby shower invitation for my friend came in the mail, I hid the invite because looking at it just made me bitter, jealous, and angry at the cards I had been dealt. The worst part was that I felt like this was our secret problem. We only shared the news with our immediate family, and while they were a wonderful support system, I never felt like it was appropriate to tell my coworkers and friends about my husband's nonexistent sperm count. So instead, I kept to myself, sinking further away from everyone else around me. When I shared my frustrations with my new gynecologist and asked for a recommendation for a urologist for my husband, she rudely told me, "You're not making a pizza; it's going to take more than fifteen minutes." No shit, we've been trying for over a year and my husband has no sperm. What a bitch.

I never got a recommendation from her, but my husband did see a urologist, whom he called Dr. Sandpaper, because of his uncomfortably rough hands. He listed off options to us, but the only one I remember was, "child-free living." WTF? I hated this doctor, too. How dare he suggest we live without children. He told us there was one procedure he could do where he would "filet" my husband's testicles and dig around looking for hidden sperm. Recovery would be painful and as Dr. Sandpaper put it, "it would feel like you were getting kicked in the balls for two weeks straight." As terrifying as it sounded, my husband was willing to give it a try. God bless his heart.

As much as I wanted kids, this just didn't seem like the best option. I suggested we search for another doctor and a second opinion. Months later we met with a new doctor at Northwestern Hospital in Chicago. He was more optimistic, his hands were smooth, and he suggested more sperm analyses before doing any horrific procedures.

Maybe there was hope. My husband did acupuncture every week and he did all the alternative remedies that were suggested to him. When the acupuncturist told him to eat goji berries, we were at the Asian supermarket within minutes. When lamb was reported to help, lamb chops were frequently on the dinner menu. Chinese herbs, check. A gluten free diet, check. No more alcohol, check. No cell phones in pockets, fertility massages, chemical free shampoo? Check, check, and check. When my husband was told to abstain from sexual activity for one month, he even had the willpower to oblige. Anything, as crazy as it may sound, was worth a try.

It was time for the next sperm analysis, and this time at a facility that had semi-private quarters with an internet connection. When they later called us with the results, it was the best news we had in years. A spattering of sperm! Who thought we'd be so excited about a handful of sperm when normally the count should be in the hundreds of millions? Things were finally looking up.

Now that we had a few sperm to work with, IVF suddenly became an option. We knew getting pregnant would not happen naturally, as did our doctors, and even our insurance company. But with the abysmal sperm count, we were approved to begin treatment right away. It was still a long shot, but there was a chance.

IVF was a train ride. Once I agreed to begin, there was no getting off. All I had to do was make it to pre-dawn appointments before work, endure daily shots, and show up to my egg retrieval and transfer. These things were uncomfortable, but I enjoyed feeling hopeful. The hardest part of the process was the emotional rollercoaster. I'd be happy to get a lot of eggs, then bummed when only one turned into a healthy embryo. I was lucky that an embryo was able to be transfered, but doubtful we would have a good outcome on our first try.

But we were lucky. We received a positive pregnancy test and after years of praying that I would get pregnant, there was finally a baby growing inside me! There was still a long, stressful road of milestones we had to pass, but I was optimistic.

I cherished every minute of those nine months. When my son was born, I cried the happiest tears I had ever cried. There was relief that he had arrived healthy and cute, and that he was actually ours. We struggled for so long and the burden of infertility was finally lifted. My soul was recovered and I was complete. I was equally emotional when we walked our son into the house for the first time. Finally, our extra bedrooms would be filled, the sledding hill would get used, and our house would no longer be lonely.

The newborn stage seemed easy because I was so overjoyed to finally have a baby. I had prepared for this; I was ready to do motherly things. Things like sleepless nights, pacing the floor all evening, and not getting to eat an uninterrupted meal didn't seem so bad because I knew what true sorrow felt like. There was nothing to be sad or stressed about; I could handle this. This was the motherhood I had planned for my entire life and I loved it.

With the help of IVF, we had another miracle baby two years later. From the moment she was just a cluster of cells in a petri dish, she has kept us on our toes. She nearly killed me in delivery, but our daughter has more than doubled our joy.

Everyday, I stare at my children's faces in disbelief because I still can't believe how lucky we are. Yes, having kids is chaotic and messy, but these two miracles are my greatest accomplishments and my greatest gifts.

I don't know if we'll have four kids like my husband and I imagined, but the two we have are perfect. Even though I'm still struggling to get pregnant again, I can see the positives that this convoluted course has shown us. I'm no longer embarrassed to talk about our infertility journey and perhaps I can provide hope for others who are struggling. I am grateful for my journey, and most importantly, that this complicated path brought us these two beautiful children. I can only appreciate what has happened and accept that, with the help of science, prayer, and grit, I have proven to myself that I was, in fact, born to be a mother.

116 Days

By Katelyn Arnold

I was meant to be a mother. I planned my life accordingly, and even chose my profession around raising a family. I married young by today's standards and left myself plenty of time to settle in to marriage, have a few years of uninterrupted fun, and then start a family. I assumed everything would go according to plan, because to be honest, my entire life had. I had a wonderful childhood, my family was pretty perfect, and I never had a defining moment of tragic loss or trauma. Sure, I had the usual teenage heartbreaks, but nothing life-altering or soul shattering. Until having those children I so desired wasn't as easy as everything else in my life had been.

There was no certain diagnosis, nothing "wrong" with me that could be determined; however, I just was not getting pregnant. After a solid year of "trying," I finally sought a professional's opinion on the matter. I attempted to regulate some slight hormonal imbalances and started seeing a fertility chiropractor. The day after Christmas in 2013, after a few years of trying, I took a pregnancy test and to my amazement, I was pregnant! One of my favorite memories to this day is jumping into bed, waking up Joe, my husband, and showing him the positive pregnancy test. We laughed, we cried, we were relieved, and we started planning for the baby immediately. Weeks went by. I felt good and we shared the news with our families. Everyone cried tears of joy and those excited moments are forever in my memory. I began to have an adorable little bump that started to appear, and at thirteen weeks, we announced our happiness to the world. I had an OB appointment at the fifteen week mark, and even though Joe was going to be out of town, I kept it because it was just routine and everything was going wonderfully. As the sonographer began the routine check, I noticed some panic in her eyes. This caused me to look at the screen and try to see what the cause of her reaction was. I could tell immediately, but I was in complete denial, and tried willing her not to speak. But it was undeniable. There was no movement where there previously had been a wiggly baby a few short weeks ago. There was no little flutter that I had come to recognize and rely on beating in the chest cavity. Then she said it. "Katelyn, I can't find a heartbeat." My world was shattered. And I was all alone.

They put me in a room and told me the doctor would be in soon. When she arrived, over ninety minutes later, she was all business. She started the conversation with "Do you want to do surgery tomorrow or Friday?" I had no idea what she was talking about because why in the world would I need surgery? She explained that the baby was too large at this point and passing it on my own could cause serious bleeding or other complications. I was in shock, alone, and blankly said, "Friday." The thought of doing this the next day was just too overwhelming and in my mental state, I just needed more time.

At this point, my husband was calling because he hadn't heard from me and was curious about how the appointment went. I broke the news to him while sobbing in my car, in a crummy parking lot full of strangers. From that point on, I was distraught at the thought that in two days, I would no longer have my baby inside of me. I sobbed in the shower while holding my bump, cried myself to sleep cradling my bump, and tried to forget that inside my adorable new bump was a dead baby. My baby.

I had the D&C on Friday, and was told we could start trying again in a few months. Little did the doctor know that it wasn't going to be that easy. This pregnancy was four years in the making, and now it was taken from us. Would it be another four years before it happened again and would it be the same horrific outcome? Being a person who shows little emotion other than happiness and confidence, I struggled with my new reality.

After suffering this loss and devastation, I had the agony of telling everyone we had lost the baby. As a high school teacher, it was so hard to return to school and face the students because they had only ever seen happy, weird Mrs. Arnold, and I knew I wouldn't be able to hold it together. Also, to add insult to injury, I had four pregnant students that semester, one of whom verbalized her distaste for her pregnancy and openly joked with friends about the various ways she was trying to end her pregnancy without having to pay for an abortion. I felt like I was about to break. For months I tried to hide my despair, but it slowly started to destroy me. Towards the end of summer, I finally admitted to my mom that I understood depression. I was there. Since I had never really even been sad before, this was a shock to my family and to myself. I started pulling out of social events because it felt like everyone around me was announcing that they were pregnant. Of course I was happy for them. I never wanted to be the person who couldn't be happy for other people. However, these joyful announcements of these couples' future families, and the general ease with which they were able to get pregnant and stay pregnant, was too much. During this time, we also got back the genetic testing results on our baby, and we discovered that we had lost a baby girl, and due to a chromosomal abnormality. We named her Claire, which was a name we decided on years ago, and tried our best to stomach what felt like the loss all over again. I shelled up in my house, my comfort zone, and tried to stay there until this terrible season of my life passed.

Then, November 17th, 2013 happened. Just as I was getting used to my new normal and relished just being home, an EF4 tornado ripped through my town and took our house with it. The neighborhood I had lived in my entire twenty-seven years of life was gone. We were safe, but the burden felt almost too heavy on my already shattered heart. I remember vividly loading up the few precious mementos we could find into a wheelbarrow with a busted front wheel, and wheeling it nine blocks down to my relatives' house. We lived at my aunt and uncle's house for a couple of weeks while my parents boarded up their broken windows, tore up their glass-filled carpet, and made their house "livable" (barely) until spring when they could start the long list of repairs. We moved in to my childhood bedroom and, just like that, started a new life.

The tornado actually proved to be a great distraction. Joe and I were busy fighting the insurance company, clearing our lot, and getting ready to rebuild. Since we didn't have a mortgage anymore, didn't have to pay rent, and my parents were generous enough to feed us and not charge us for groceries, water, electricity, or anything, we were able to stow away some money and start paying for a fertility doctor.

After our first meeting with Dr. G, I felt immensely better. We had a plan. We would try X and if that didn't work in three months, we would try Y and if that didn't work in three months, we would try Z. I left our first appointment knowing that one way or another, we were going to be parents.

We started with exploratory surgery. There was nothing identifiably wrong with me and according to our doctor, my husband had "super sperm." I started taking Clomid, but of course was the .2% that had hallucinations and started seeing "trailers." After one week, we were already on to the next plan. I started injections and we were going to try IUI (intrauterine insemination). So everyday, I gave myself shots to grow my eggs and a shot of heparin for a clotting disorder. I went to the fertility doctor's office every other day to have an internal ultrasound to check the size of my eggs, and when it was deemed that they were large enough, I was given a "trigger shot" to make the eggs drop. I was then inseminated and we prayed for the best.

Not pregnant.

Dr. G and the nurses tried their best to be encouraging. "It only has a 20% success rate. Give it a few more tries." So I began giving myself the shots again, participating in the constant internal exams, and hoping and praying it worked this month.

Not pregnant.

The steps repeated themselves again, and the result was, again, the same.

Not pregnant.

At this point, I was breaking. Months of injections, thousands of dollars thrown away, the bruises all over my body from the heparin. It was physically, emotionally, and spiritually draining. I decided to give it one more try and then we were going to have to explore another option. My nurse recommended I try acupuncture in conjunction with my treatments because she had heard a lot of recent success stories when the two were paired together. I figured I had nothing to lose, except for another thousand dollars, and started getting acupuncture treatments three times a week. The steps repeated, the insemination occurred, and now it was the brutal fourteen day waiting period again. This time *felt* different. I was in agony and felt like something was wrong with my ovaries and my uterus. They felt heavy, twisted, painful, and I started to get some serious abdominal swelling within days of the insemination. I knew something sinister was going on, but I also knew it probably meant the outcome this time was different. Sure enough, a blood test on the fourteenth day confirmed something was indeed different. I was pregnant.

We were excited but cautious this time. I tried not to feel it, get excited about it, or make any plans. I knew what it felt like to have those dreams shattered, so this time I was going to be smart about it and be prepared for the loss. Humans are funny creatures. We act like these defense mechanisms will honestly make a difference, like if I lost this child it wouldn't be as hurtful because I was "prepared" for it. But I was preparing for it. Everyday, I was waiting for the floor to fall out. I also was in *pain*. The pain increasingly got worse. I was no stranger to pain, and even prided myself on my high tolerance. I finally admitted that something wasn't normal because sixteen days after the insemination, I could barely stand up. After another internal exam, it was concluded that I had Ovarian Hyperstimulation Syndrome. Basically, I had too many hormones in my system due to the injections, my ovaries had swollen to the size of grapefruits, and they were at risk of twisting. I was the rare reaction where the hormones from pregnancy were actually feeding the ovaries and making them larger by the day. I was put on bed rest and told I could not work, could not be on my feet, and had to wait until my ovaries returned to their natural state. To make matters worse, a new school year was starting the following week and I was going to have to tell the administration that I was pregnant and having complications at least three or four months before we would have told anyone. How ridiculous would I sound: "Hi, I am *16 days* pregnant and can't come to school because I am on bed rest, sorry!"

My absence lasted almost three weeks and I returned to work. Aside from random bleeding and constant fear, my pregnancy ticked along. During our first ultrasound, we were in for another surprise. The doctor said, "There's one, oh there's another.

Let's see if we see any more..." At that moment, my husband and I looked at each other and then said, "MORE?" We had eight eggs drop during that IUI session, therefore we had the chance of having eight babies. During the three previous failed IUI attempts, I had between six and eight eggs drop every time, and none of them got fertilized. So for a few long seconds we were preparing for a reality with at least twins, potentially oc-tuplets. After close examination, it was determined we were expecting twins and we prepared to have a "complicated/high risk pregnancy." Truer words had never been spoken.

Complicated doesn't even begin to describe what my pregnancy journey was like. I had just about everything go wrong that could go wrong. On two separate occasions, I ended up in the emergency room and once was even told that I lost both babies. During that ER experience, after losing so much blood that I almost passed out, all of my fears were realized as the doctor said, "We see fetal matter and can't find heartbeats. You need to accept your reality, go home, and take care of yourself." I felt in my bones that he was wrong. I would feel it if my babies were gone, even if I hadn't even felt them move yet. I was their mother. I fought to stay at the hospital and have an internal ultrasound done by radiology

146

so I could see for myself that their hearts weren't beating and that they were gone. The doctor was heartless, rude, and treated me like an idiot; however, I stuck to my convictions. He lectured me and told me I was going to waste hospital resources and my money, but if I wanted to, I could wait all night and waste everyone's time. And that is exactly what I did. My husband was on a flight to China, and I was not going to call him and tell him we lost the babies without being 100% certain. After waiting all night with the weight of what the doctor said the outcome would be, I was taken up to radiology. I couldn't see the screen, and the ultrasound technician wouldn't say what the findings were without having the doctor read the report. I started crying and begged her to put me out of my misery. I told her the doctor had already told me my babies were gone and this was just my insane need for confirmation. She then broke protocol and said, "I don't know why the doctor told you that, your babies are perfectly fine." She turned the screen around and there in front of me were two beating hearts, two wiggly, very alive babies, and my heart and sanity restored.

Obviously, hospitals don't discharge you until the doctor has formally read the report and relayed it's findings to the patient.

At this point I was downright angry and when he came in with his smug-ass attitude, I have never wanted to insult a human being more. I was cold, rude, and told him that I hoped this was a lesson in his bedside manner. If I had listened to him and left the hospital like he suggested, I would have assumed my babies were dead and would have fallen into despair and potentially would have lost them from lack of care. I wrote a strongly-worded letter to the hospital and later crucified him on the aftercare survey.

After following up with my doctor, it was confirmed that I had a very large intrauterine tear. When the babies were pushed against it, the bleeding was controlled, but if they shifted positions and exposed the tear, I lost large amounts of blood. This periodically happened for several weeks and warranted another hospital visit. Little did I know that the next time I went to the hospital, I wouldn't be leaving.

November had begun, our house was being rebuilt, and we just found out a few weeks prior that we were expecting two girls! My husband had to leave for another business trip to Europe, but since we were still living with my parents due to the tornado, I had plenty of people to look after me. I wasn't feeling great and spoke to my mom about my concerns. We rationalized that if I could fall asleep and stay asleep, there was no need to call the doctor. If I was still struggling with pressure and pain, I would either head to the hospital or call the doctor in the morning. I still was experiencing weird bands of pressure, but the pain that accompanied it was gone, so I wasn't concerned.

When I got to work one day, I was talking to my friend and she calmly told me that I should call my doctor because what I was describing was exactly how she felt when she went into labor. I sort of laughed it off and called my doctor expecting to hear her say that it wasn't alarming and to keep her posted if things acted up. Instead, she told me to come in right away. So I quickly arranged a sub, told the school I would be back in an hour, and headed to the doctor's office. Once there, they did an internal ultrasound and said, "Katelyn, you're in labor. We need to get you to the hospital right away." I had just reached twenty weeks that morning, so this was very alarming. They asked if I needed an ambulance to take me and told me I needed to call my parents and my husband. I remember saying, "Oh, so this is a situation? You aren't just being overcautious here?" They assured me that they weren't and if I was going to drive myself, they were going to notify the hospital and have someone waiting with a wheelchair in the parking lot as I arrived. So I hopped in my car, called my mom, and told her to meet me at the hospital because the doctor said that I was in labor. When I got there, a team was waiting with a wheelchair and said, "You must be Katelyn. Sit down, we've got to go!" I was confused, scared, and honestly didn't know what to think. One of Joe's friends from college, luckily, was the first nurse I saw. She got me changed, hooked up to countless monitors, gave me an IV, and explained what was happening. I told her that I couldn't reach Joe and she assured me she would take care of contacting him. My mom arrived just as I was being wheeled to another part of the hospital. As we all boarded the elevator a nurse joked, "Well it looks like you have family around so at least someone will bring you Thanksgiving dinner in a few weeks!" I thought she was joking. I responded with something like, "Thanksgiving?! I better not be here that long!" to which she responded, "Honey, if you're lucky, you'll be here for Thanksgiving, Christmas, New Years, Valentines Day, St. Patrick's Day, and potentially Easter." The gravity of the situation became clear.

The first day of my hospital stay introduced me to magnesium sulfate. This is what I would refer to as "devil juice" for the next eleven weeks. Magnesium sulfate relaxes small muscle tissue, which in turn relaxes the uterus enough to stop or slow contractions. While the desired outcome is good, keeping the baby inside, the side effects are horrible. I felt like the drunkest I'd ever been, simultaneously mixed with the most hungover I'd ever been. I got double or triple vision and my veins hurt. I felt as though I was literally burning from the inside out. When nurses gave me a bolus (a high dosage of IV medication to get a large amount into my system as fast as they could), I got very *very* sick. I was shaking, vomiting, hallucinating, and felt like I was dying a slow, burning, torturous death.

Since magnesium sulfate relaxes your small muscle tissues, it relaxed my bladder too much, and I lost the ability to empty it. I had to be catheterized and the cath remained for the next nine weeks. The first two or three days of this, I barely recall. I was in and out of consciousness due to the "mag" and when the bolus started to wear off, I was brought into the reality of my situation. Joe had somehow made it back from Europe, and I had a large number of doctors, nurses, and techs in and out of my room at all hours of the day and night. After day three, I was still contracting, my cervix was continuing to shorten, and the doctors decided on a last ditch effort plan to keep me pregnant and keep my babies alive. They were going to perform a surgery called a cerclage and were literally going to stitch my cervix shut in an effort to keep the babies in.

Prepping for the surgery was scary. Doctors didn't let Joe go in with me, and I was still horribly ill from the mag. And I was scared. They gave me a spinal and paralyzed me from the chest down. Then they strapped my arms down (Jesus-style, as I call it, like I was hanging on a crucifix), and I willed my strong mental game to carry me through. I just remember begging for water, or an ice chip or a damp cloth or *anything* with moisture to be put in my mouth. Mag gave me extreme cotton mouth and I felt like I was choking to death. Add paralyzation, sickness, physical restraints, and extreme thirst together, and I felt like I might really be dying. This journey kept teaching me about myself: I thought I was strong, but there were limits to my strength. And it was day three.

Surgery went well, my cervix was stitched shut, and I was informed that I would be not only be on prolonged bed rest, but that I would need to be in Trendelenburg position (head towards the ground, feet elevated above) for the foreseeable future.

It was weird laying virtually upside down for long periods of time. My head felt like it was going to explode, which caused me to cry, which then made my head *really* feel like it was going to explode. To suggest that my bed rest journey was traumatic is a gross understatement. Every day felt like a torture chamber. It was either new IV day, new catheter day, or new scary procedure day, all while mostly upside down. The weight of the situation was always heavy. I was only twenty weeks pregnant. Babies can *possibly* survive at twenty-four weeks, but with serious lifelong complications. Even if I made it a month, which no one realistically thought I could, my babies may not survive. Twenty-eight weeks was always the goal, and in my mind, the unattainable goal. At magical twenty-eight weeks, the heart, brain and lungs are developed enough that the babies might have a chance at a "normal" life. How was I supposed to endure this for that long? Especially with no guarantee that everything would work out in the end?

Days came and went. Some days, shit hit the fan (literally). Other days, the torture was my new normal. In just a short year,

I truly had a whole new perspective on life. The luxuries of my life like running water, heat, electricity, and comfort were taken from me in a fluke tornado. The immediate days after the tornado truly felt dystopian. We were under Marshall Law, I had no belongings, we had no heat and no running water. We begged people on social media to meet us with gas for our chainsaws, for plywood, for water and food. We had to trek across town, through police checkpoints with the possibility of not being let back in, just to take shower. And now here I was, trapped, under a different kind of Marshall Law, unable to do anything I wanted, including taking a shower. I wasn't allowed to sit up in my bed, let alone use my toilet. So I laid in an uncomfortable hospital bed, shitting in a bedpan, a catheter hanging out of my lady region, with people shoving various objects up my vagina daily and NEVER getting to wash any of it off. This was my biggest struggle. I have super long, thick hair and it gets greasy after a few days. The nurses concocted a way to wash my hair while I was lying in bed, with a pool float around my head, pitchers of water to rise into the pool float, which was then emptied into a garbage and dumped down the drain in the bathroom. It worked but never well enough. It was impossible to get all of the shampoo/conditioner out of my hair, which in turn, became itchy as it dried. I felt like I had lice my entire stay. I would beg people to shave me (yes, all of me), and would literally cry if on scheduled bath day, I didn't get one. I battled infections and was breaking the hospital's catheter "rule" every day. A patient should only be cathed for forty-eight hours. I was cathed for weeks.

The catheter became my second battle. Without it, my contractions intensified, my stitch threatened to tear, and the babies could come. With it, I had bladder infections, which intensified my contractions, as well. I had my catheter changed every four days. After using one for so long, my urethra began to grow around the catheter, and changing it became more and more painful. On the morning of cath change days, I woke up with a sense of dread, knowing I was going to scream in pain. IV days became bad too. I was running out of good veins since they change the IV every three days, and I had bruises, bandaids, and medical tape residue all over my body. Bed baths never got all of the tape residue off, so sticky and itchy became part of my general state.

I was sticky, itchy, greasy, dirty, hairy, infected, and still contracting every two to ten minutes. I was tied down to the bed in three places: my leg pumps to maintain circulation and prevent blood clots, my catheter, and my IV. As someone who cannot stand to be restrained, being held to a bed in three places, twenty-four hours a day started to take a toll on my mental state. So did the lack of fresh air, another luxury I previously took for granted.

I had a little window, but it became taunting to *see* outside and not be able to *breathe* outside. Hospital air was so dry, the mag gave me cottonmouth all the time, and a few times I felt almost a panic. I begged the staff to roll my bed outside just so I could take a few deep breaths of the cold air. It never happened.

I tried to remain positive, because against all odds, I was still pregnant. When I was in agony, I would look at the little cross in the corner of the room with Jesus hanging on it and say to myself, "If he could do that, I can do this." My faith got stronger. My relationships with people deepened. I was so vulnerable chained to a bed, in the same room, without reprieve. I was at the mercy of whomever walked through the door. This became a challenge for me because although I wanted my family and friends to keep me company, I didn't want to make small talk with people from my past. I had *the most random* people just walk through my door to see me. Old acquaintances from high school, people I worked with professionally, parents of old friends, people from my church that I didn't know well. Virtual strangers would walk through the door when I was naked, when I was getting probed, when I was shitting in my bedpan, when I was having a bad mag moment and vomiting off the side of my bed, even when I was sleeping (yes, I woke up on a few occasions to see someone I once "knew" sitting in the chair next to me, staring at me). They came out of the goodness of their hearts, but it often left me embarrassed and angry. I felt they didn't know me well enough to earn a conversation with me when I was at my most vulnerable.

One of the most common comments I heard from the "outsiders" was, "Man, it would be kind of nice to not have to go to work and be able to take naps and watch Netflix all day." My typical response was "Fuck you." I didn't actually say this, but I wanted to. This wasn't some vacation. This wasn't your typical bed rest in the comforts of your home, with your family by your side to help you, where you get to relax and wait for the last couple weeks of pregnancy to slip by. Not to discredit anyone on home bed rest, but I had done that for a few weeks and the two experiences were vastly different. This wasn't even the typical hospital bed rest situation that I believe most of my visitors thought they were walking in to. I wasn't passing time and hoping for a visitor, able to get out of bed just to use the toilet or take a quick shower. I was in actual pain, dirty, and my room often smelled like shit (honestly). And here my random visitors were just walking in to my smell factory and it was humiliating.

I was angry at the situation, as I was just an incubator, unable to move, and my body started to deteriorate at a rate I never expected. For one, I couldn't watch Netflix or read all day because my vision was impaired due to the magnesium. I had double or triple vision and watching things or reading made me even more nauseous. Also, I *never* got sleep. Anyone who has been in a hospital knows that nurses, doctors, techs, maintenance workers, custodians, cafeteria deliverers, flower deliverers, dietitians, etc. are in your room at all hours of the day. Vitals were taken every three hours, so on a good day, I had three consecutive hours of sleep. However, good days rarely happened. This sleep deprivation just added to my laundry list of ailments.

Thanksgiving came and went. Christmas came and went. My cousin's wife put it perfectly when she visited on Christmas. She said, "Holy shit, you are in the exact same position as you were when we visited on Thanksgiving. When I think of all I've done and how much time has actually passed, this creeps me out." It creeped me out, too. Through all the bad, however, there was some serious good happening too. My relationships got so much deeper.

God truly knew what he was doing when he blessed me with Joe Arnold. My husband was the best caregiver, supporter, and entertainer that I could have ever hoped for. Of my eighty-one days in the hospital, he didn't sleep next to me only three (and two of those were because he was in Europe when this started and was trying to get home to me). His six-foot-three body curled onto that rickety, old hospital cot night after night. My parents, brother, and sister came every single day. My aunt came almost everyday and always brought something delicious and luxurious. Our good family friends were constantly popping in to converse, letting me vent, and keeping me company. My close friends checked in and stopped by to help me laugh a little. The nurses, techs, and doctors became like family and my room became the fun room to hang out in for the hospital staff. I discovered My People during this time, and I knew regardless of how this turned out, I would always have this support system.

Shortly after New Year's Day, two months into this nightmare, things changed. Since I was twenty-eight weeks and three days, and doctors were feeling good about how the girls were growing. The catheter came out, I got to stand up, I was able to SHOWER, and I got to see what my belly looked like in a mirror. It was the morale boost I needed and that twenty-eight week mark mentally shifted my world. My pregnancy finally felt real, I felt like my babies would actually survive, and I felt that Joe and I were going to be parents. What I didn't expect was how weak I had become. When I tried to get to the shower, I wasn't able to walk on my own. My muscles had atrophied so badly that I couldn't support my weight. I knew extensive physical therapy would be in my future, but I had no idea the toll this experience would take on my body. I still was confined to my bed after that brief field trip to the bathroom, and at thirty weeks, the magnesium sulfate ended. Most people are on mag no more than forty-eight hours. I had been on it for ten weeks. Doctors did not have any research as to what the long-term mag effects would be on me or the babies. We just had to have faith that everything would be fine and realize that without it, I wouldn't have my babies. So whatever the outcome was, it was better than the alternative.

I didn't do well off the mag, or without the catheter. Retraining a bladder that hadn't had to work on its own for almost nine weeks was tough. I constantly felt like I couldn't empty and had persistent weird sensations. Without the mag, my labor was progressing back to dangerous levels and they gave me a couple of corticosteroid injections to hopefully improve the girls' lungs, in the case that I were to deliver. My cervical stitches tore (yes, that was as painful that it sounds) due to contractions and within an hour of the tearing, I started to go into active labor again.

The evening of thirty weeks and six days, I knew something wasn't right. I was in agony (a different agony than normal) and I woke Joe up to go get the nurses. The doctor came in and they were moving me to labor and delivery. They gave me another IV bolus of magnesium sulfate and I was in bad shape. The burning again, the sickness, the vomiting, except this time it wasn't working. Since I hit thirty-one weeks that morning and one of the girls was breech, my doctor informed me that I was going to be having a C-section that afternoon. For the last ten weeks, I was praying for this experience to be over and now that it almost was, I was terrified.

We called our parents, and the hospital informed us that we needed to clean out the room that had become home the past three months. Joe and my family feverishly threw everything into suitcases and I got prepped for the C-section. I was in a lot of pain and my contractions were becoming unbearable. One of the babies wasn't handling the contractions well and I got whisked away, scared of not only my future, but also those of the two other people I was about to bring into this world. We had come so far and now that we were on the brink of becoming actual parents, I was still thinking worst-case-scenario in an effort to preserve my heart.

Joe went with the NICU doctors and was shown the room where they would take the girls immediately after they were removed. I was taken to the OR and given a spinal. I hadn't been vertical in so long that the act of sitting up straight gave me the worst sense of vertigo. I was super disoriented, dizzy, and then came the cold sweats. I dove directly into the chest of a nurse and then threw up down her boobs. Add it to the list of my never-ending humiliation. After the puke-fest, I got into position, Joe arrived, my doctor arrived, and we were ready to go. The procedure didn't take long and although I was vomiting the entire time, the next few moments were otherworldly.

I felt a weird pressure, and then an even stranger release and then heard an actual little cry. I don't remember thinking anything except "She's alive! One of my babies is actually alive." They brought her over so I could see her, but only for a few seconds. They put her in an incubator and whisked her away. Seconds later, there was that same pressure, followed by a release and baby girl number two came out. She wasn't crying and was immediately taken from the room, along with my husband. A nurse did come back in and say something to the effect of, "You have two daughters: Grace Ann and Harper Jo. Congratulations!" I remember thinking, "Holy shit, Joe just named them!" completely forgetting that we had decided on names earlier. I didn't know what was going on, was overwhelmed with the whole situation, and was so sick and delirious that I don't really remember what happened over the next few hours. Apparently, I was closed up, taken to recovery, and I took awhile to come out of it all. In the meantime, Joe went with the girls and was with baby number two, Harper, as they worked on her. The girls were taken to the NICU and placed in the critical section. They were in separate rooms, but in the same "neighborhood." It turns out that night I was wheeled down to see them, but aside from seeing the pictures my husband took, I have no recollection of it.

I was in the weeds while recovering. I hadn't been vertical for three months, I had severe muscle atrophy, I couldn't walk, and I just had a C-section (which C-section was barely noticeable when I took account of all of the issues I was having). Joe, still sleeping by my side, would wake up, take care of me, and then head down to the NICU. He wanted to be with the babies every minute of every day and for that I love him. I, however, did not feel that way. I was exhausted. It had been virtually three months without multiple interruptions during sleep, I felt like my body was shutting down, and I was in the depths of trying to pump, walk, poop, and get my mind right again. Plus, I couldn't walk down to the NICU and had to wait for my medications before I could go anyway, so I was constantly relying on hospital transport to wheel me to the other side of the hospital, just to see my babies.

The NICU was depressing. Where Joe loved being in the rooms with the girls, I hated it. It was dim, quiet, and we couldn't hold or touch our babies. We just stared at them in their incubators and waited for them to get bigger and healthier. So much waiting. I was struggling because I was not attached to the babies at all. All of those motherly feelings I expected to feel did not exist. I didn't have this overwhelming love for them and felt like an inadequate mother. Joe was obsessed with them and hated every second he wasn't with them. What was wrong with me? I think I had spent so much time preparing to lose them, that when they were actually there in front of me, I was completely disconnected.

It took me a week to get discharged from the hospital, and I still wasn't able to walk, so I left in a wheelchair. Since we didn't have a house to go home to, Joe and I headed back to my parents' place, while the girls remained in the hospital. Leaving the girls behind destroyed Joe. And while it should have torn me up too, it did not. I was ready to get the hell out of the hospital and I didn't want to go back. It had been eighty-four days since I had last been at home, actually showered, ate with my family, slept in a comfortable bed, and snuggled with my dog, Marley. I was in heaven during that drive home and knew that once I was "home," I was going to get back to feeling like me.

Joe had to return to work and it was up to me to keep him posted with the daily progress reports from the doctors. He would text me early and ask, "What did the doctors say at rounds this morning?" and I felt like a piece-of-shit mom because I wasn't at the hospital yet. He was loving and supportive and even though he never vocalized it, I felt like this frustrated him. He would be there at 5:00am if he could, he would be there all day if he didn't have to work, and here I was still at my parents' house, with no hustle in me to get to the hospital. I was a prisoner there for so long, and I didn't want to wake up at the crack of dawn, only to sit in the NICU rooms alone all day. Plus, I couldn't drive and couldn't walk myself to the NICU from the drop off point, so I had to inconvenience my parents or other family members and friends each and every day. Eventually, we got into a routine and someone would take me, wheel me to the girls' rooms, and Joe would join me after work. We would hang out together until about 8:00 or 9:00pm and then go back home.

Each day, the girls would make progress. Eventually, they got moved into the same room, which was a game changer. Until that point, Joe would sit in one room, I would sit in the other, and then we would switch every so often. Now we could at least hang out together in a room, so that made me feel much less lonely. We got close with nurses and began to get used to this whole parenting thing. Nurses would let us change their diapers, which took some real skills inside of an incubator. They got the girls out a couple times a day to do skin-to-skin, which was really the only time we got to hold them. My milk supply was struggling because not only was I not really able to hold my babies to stimulate production, but I couldn't put them to breast more than once a day because they had to monitor exactly how much milk they were consuming. I was pumping with all of my might, every two hours, but still wasn't producing enough. We supplemented with donor milk and the girls got fed through their feeding tube every few hours.

With two babies, we were always dealing with something with one of them. They struggled with feeding, bradycardias, regulating body temperature, abnormal blood draws or scans. The day that really threw us for a loop was around the thirty-four week mark (three weeks after birth). They had routine brain scans since they were born prematurely and we expected everything to come back normal. Instead, we were informed that Grace's looked good, but Harper had some abnormal shadowing. They didn't know what that meant at this point, but warned us that she might have cerebral palsy or another developmental disorder because of it. I felt like the wind was knocked out of me. Here we were, after everything, finally parents. Now this.

Immediately, I saw Harper, possibly unable to walk, run or participate in everyday activities, while Grace is mobile, healthy and most likely harboring this unresolved guilt for the rest of her life. Harper envious and angry of what Grace has, Grace enjoying her blessings but crippled with guilt. I was devastated. After follow-up scans, meetings with the doctor, and being ignorant enough to turn to the Internet in the midst of my fear, it was pretty much too early to determine anything and more waiting began. I was already struggling physically and mentally, I was struggling to attach, to balance home and hospital life, and now I had a bullshit *maybe* diagnosis? This was a thief of joy. Even the little glimmers of happiness in that NICU room and the little bits of joy that I would feel had an extra layer of worry attached to them. I would sit in front of Harper's incubator and cry, while looking at her little under-developed legs and try to see if I could tell a difference between hers and Grace's. I found myself pouring more love, more energy, and more of my heart into Harper because of her possible life-changing diagnosis. Then came the guilt. Why wasn't I doing that with Grace? It was because Grace seemed stronger, progressing quicker, and would most likely have a much easier life. Grace was off the feeding tubes before Harper, she was out of the incubator quicker than Harper, and it looked like she would be going home before Harper. I was so torn.

The weeks came and went. We settled into our routine, balanced our time between "home" and the hospital, continued to monitor progress on the rebuilding of our house, and tried to celebrate the little victories. Harper was catching up to Grace, we were making progress with feeding and body temperature regulation, and the doctors and nurses started mentioning potentially heading home in the near future. Once again, it was this weird feeling that could mostly be equated to bittersweet. Just like when I was at the brink and dying for my pregnancy journey to end, I didn't feel ready for it when the time came. Now, we were almost done with the hospital and the NICU, which should be exhilarating, yet I was dreading the end to it all. But we knew how to do everything we needed to do for these babies, from feeding, bathing, medicating, and watching for the occasional bradycardia that Harper would have during feedings. So, on February 28th, 2015, after 116 consecutive days at the hospital, we were headed home together.

We were like freaking machines. Due to their tiny size, the girls had to eat every two or three hours. By the time we changed them, fed them, medicated them, burped them, and got them back down, it was time to wake them up again. It was a never-ending blur of diapers, bottles, washing bottles, pumping, cleaning the pump and parts, mixing the supplemental milk, labeling everything, charting ounces consumed, weighing wet diapers, etc., etc., etc. It was impossible to sleep because even when we did everything on the list and got them down for a bit, they never really both slept at the same time. The luxury that parents of singletons take for granted is the, "I'll do this feeding, you sleep through this one." That is just not possible with preemie twins. Even if I could do all of that on my own to both of them, I would never get it done in time before I would have to do it all again. And to complicate things further, I couldn't do my pumping during the time of changing, feeding, medicating, and burping, so when Joe could maybe grab a few moments of shut eye, I had to hook up the pump to milk myself. I was exhausted and losing my mind. Luckily, my mom and Joe are insomniacs, so they functioned on very little sleep and didn't mind late night feedings and "the routine." There was always one feeding where I could skip and I would grab my dog, go to the depths of the cold, dark basement and pass out for two whole hours before the pumping had to begin again.

I couldn't skip a pumping. Every two hours, my phone alarm went off and I hooked myself up. Since I had two babies to feed (and the NICU doctors stressed how important breast milk was for preemies), and had all the cards stacked against me in the breastfeeding world, I had to stimulate my breasts every two hours. I gave birth nine weeks early, I was heavily medicated far longer than any mother should be, I had a C-section, I had two mouths to feed, I wasn't allowed to put them to breast, I had so many exterior stressors with the house rebuild and the health issues of the girls, and I came from a long line of biologically inept breastfeeders. If that doesn't scream "doomed for failure," I don't know what does. I was slowly but surely falling into despair. This wasn't fun. It wasn't how I imagined it to be. My body was a wreck and I was struggling with after-effects of my bed rest. I swore to myself I would NEVER complain about anything to do with pregnancy or my babies because I prayed for so many years and begged God to give me the opportunity to be a mother. I hated the parents who bitched on Facebook about how tired they were because their babies weren't sleeping well. I vowed to never be that person. Yet, here I was, hooked up to the pump for the billionth time, and crying from exhaustion, frustration, and sadness. Joe came in and asked what was wrong and I couldn't even explain it. It all felt wrong. I felt robbed of the experience. Joe in all of his wisdom said, "Kate, you have everything you ever prayed for." And that was the truth. I felt guilty but this snapped me back to reality. I knew I had to make some changes.

The first change was to swallow my pride, admit I had failed at breastfeeding, and to be okay with that. I was not the mother who dreamed of breastfeeding and was going to strictly breast-feed no matter what. Selfishly, I wanted to breastfeed to help me get back to my pre-baby size and save money in the formula department. Yes, it was also good for the baby, but due to science, so was formula. My siblings and I were formula fed and we are all tall, healthy, smart, active people with no allergies. I had made it nine whole weeks and had made it to the girls' due date. My milk had been depleting for weeks, even with the extra pumping and other means to try to stimulate my lactation. The girls had gotten the colostrum, which was the most important, and they were growing like weeds. We spoke to their doctor, got them on the formula they needed, and I said goodbye to pumping. I cannot describe the difference this made in my life. I was HUMAN again. I was a tired human, but I was me again. I felt like my baby blues washed away, I got some actual sleep, and really started to attach to Grace and Harper. I was finding joy in motherhood and didn't feel like I was just surviving.

We were a couple months removed from the hospital and our house was nearing completion. Joe was chomping at the bit to move back home and tackle parenthood together. I was dreading it. I didn't know how we would survive without all of the helping hands we were blessed enough to enjoy since living at my parents' house. Plus, Joe would have to go to work, and I would be at home by myself. With two infants. I was in a groove, felt confident enough to keep them alive, and had developed a strong attachment to them, but now I was supposed to do this all day by myself?!

On May 8th, 2015, we finally moved home. It was eighteen months post tornado, and now we were a family of four. It was weird and overwhelming, but also something that I was able to handle. My family stopped by to help with feedings and due to my back issues, someone stopped by everyday to lift the girls into the crib for nap time and came over to lift them out when they woke up. I was so thankful to have family that didn't hesitate to interrupt their day to stop by to literally put my babies in a crib and then come back to lift them out. Being dependent on other people is just so freaking humbling. Once again, time passed in one tired blur, but life was good, and Joe and I felt like we were actually enjoying ourselves more and more each month.

After all that I endured to create and keep alive my children, I have struggled to find adequate words to describe what mother-hood means to me. Was it everything I hoped and dreamed of? No. It just isn't what I had imagined because pre-children, I was incapable of grasping the abstract concept of what being a mom actually means. I feel like I am still me, and I still nurture the person that I am and was before they came along. I still value my relationship with my husband just as much as I did before, and against what everyone says, I still put him and us first. Our girls are healthy, happy, silly, smart, and strong-willed. They know what love is because they see it between Joe and me and they feel the love we pour into them everyday. They are the best of both of us and are true miracles. I longed to be a mother so much and my heart truly is complete because of them. I hope as they get older and learn about their journey into this world, they can grasp how much I fought for them and can feel my love on a different level. As they grow and potentially pursue motherhood themselves, I hope they let go of the expectations of pregnancy and motherhood and just embrace their individual journeys for what they are.

When I reflect on my motherhood journey, the biggest influence in my success was my relationship with God. I had a strong faith before, but after this experience I feel much closer to God. I remember hearing people say, "God will never give you more than you can handle." I always found that saying a little strange because truthfully, God can throw an array of awful circumstances your way and you really have no choice but to handle them. There isn't really an alternative. In my life, I felt like God kept throwing these difficult circumstances my way and I felt victimized and asked, "Why me? What did I do to deserve this?" But as I have matured and have grown to understand God more, I have developed the philosophy that God does not make bad things happen to people. Bad things randomly happen in life, but that is when God is there to help navigate through them. I know God was there the entire time because through all of the muck, there were good things that came out of each and every heartbreak and difficult situation. Although saying something positive came out of our late-term miscarriage and loss of our baby girl, as well as a six-year battle with infertility, seems wrong, I truly feel that without those circumstances, I wouldn't have been able to fight for Grace and Harper the way I did.

My hospitalization was physically, mentally, spiritually, and emotionally intense, and has had lasting implications on my health. But if I hadn't experienced the miscarriage and the subsequent yearning to be a parent, I wouldn't have had the resolve to fight for the twins. Although the tornado was awful and traumatic, it put us where we needed to be, which was at a house full of helpful people. We saved money to afford fertility treatments, our dog was not just left alone while we were in the hospital for three months, and my family was there to help with the girls and my recovery. If I hadn't gone into the hospital on the exact day that I did, Dr. Renfroe would not have been the doctor on duty. She was the only doctor of the three that would have kept me on the magnesium sulfate and catheter as long as she did, which proved to be the only way I was able to carry to the girls to viability. Even my bed rest turned out to be a positive experience in retrospect. The impact it had on my relationships can never truly be described. I got to really know everyone I loved and truly felt the effects of unconditional love. It strengthened my relationship with my immediate family, my aunts and uncles, my friends, my coworkers and most importantly, my husband.

We were dealt some tough cards in a short amount of time and Joe's love for me never wavered. He was there. He held my hand as I screamed in pain from a procedure (you can't knock a pregnant girl out with anesthesia, after all), he cleaned up my shit when it happened to get places it shouldn't have, and he helped me battle pink eye when said shit happened to get in my eye (twice). He put medicine in my gross unshowered vagina daily, he massaged my greasy body, and bathed me when the nurse didn't get to it. He made me laugh, brought me my favorite foods, and on two separate occasions even evaded hospital staff and cameras to sneak my precious dog to my room when I was on the brink of losing it. He didn't just say he loved me, he showed me he loved me, regardless of how ugly, dirty, angry, sad, medicated, and mentally broken I was. He took our marriage vows to heart and proved that "through sickness and in health" wasn't just some bullshit line. Most people don't get to experience the tough parts of failing health resulting in the "caregiver" status until later in their marriages. We were given the opportunity earlier than most and I am thankful for that. That period of time proved to me that regardless of life's uncertainties, we will be able handle it together.

My experience is something that I look back on with fondness, and weirdly enough some of my best moments of my life occurred within all of the tribulations. I love the person this experience has made me. I know I can survive anything. This has made me a better mother, a more loving spouse, a more caring teacher, and, in general, a better human being. After all this, when things get difficult, I now know that not only do I have my family and Joe to carry me through, but I also have the big Guy in the Sky orchestrating even the toughest moments into the most worthwhile lessons. And I have my two precious girls. And what else is there?

A Tub Full of Medicine

By Marie Moretti

I met my husband, Michael, at the age of thirty one. I hit the jackpot, as he is super sweet, an excellent cook, he's caring and thoughtful, he loves dogs, and he embraces and loves my family. And his family is simply wonderful beyond words. We fell in love quickly and got married a year from our first date. In letters that we wrote to each other while we were dating, we always included, "you will be an amazing father one day," or "you will make the most wonderful mother." So, it was obvious that we both wanted children. What wasn't obvious were the trials and tribulations in trying to grow our family that were about to rock us to our core.

Six months after we were married, we began trying. We bought a basal thermometer to monitor my ovulation. We read articles about which times of the month were most likely to result in a boy or girl. I visited my gynecologist and spoke to her about my age and my concerns about not getting pregnant after the first months of trying. She was not too concerned because I was only thirty two. However, six months after that visit she put me on a regimen of fertility pills and gels. She didn't monitor me or guide me other than that. The medicine made me extremely angry and emotional. I broke out so terribly that my pimples would literally pop by themselves. It was awful. I was blessed enough to have a husband who didn't see the pimples, who didn't get offended by the emotional outbursts. He just supported me. But I stopped the medicines in the second month because I knew it wasn't right for my body.

Due to the lack of concern and help from my gynecologist, we began reading online reviews for fertility doctors in our area. We chose the one who seemed to be the best fit. We didn't know what to expect but they did a battery of tests and ended up telling us all of the stuff we didn't want to hear. "You have premature ovarian failure. Your sperm count and quality aren't what we would like. You have a polyp that will need to be removed through surgery. Hurry and sign these papers even though we haven't explained to you what we are going to do and oh yes, we are asking you to sign them as we draw your blood. Here's the pen, sign now." To make matters worse, this fertility place called me when I was at work (I am a teacher) with minutes to spare before my students came back into my classroom and a nurse casually told me OVER THE PHONE that I might have a brain tumor. "I am sorry, what did you just say? Aren't you supposed to be talking about my fertility not my brain?" And who in her right mind has a nurse call and literally say, "You might have a brain tumor. Ma'am are you still there. Are you ok?" Of course, I am not ok. You just told me that I might have a brain tumor and twenty-six first graders are coming back into my classroom and I am supposed to teach them. As soon as my students left for the day, I panicked and called my husband who saved me from going into a complete meltdown.

This was one of the most terrifying times of my life, and I am certain, my husband's, too. And that was just the beginning of our infertility journey. I got an MRI as soon as I could, which was not pleasant. Even though it was a horrifying experience, it was a relief to find out I did not have a brain tumor. While I was glad I was ok, I was enraged at that nurse.

We switched fertility doctors. More of the same heartbreaking news. So we switched again to get another perspective. Same heartbreaking news. Denial is very strong when the news cuts so deep. We did whatever these doctors told us to do. Never had I felt so blind and helpless. We were to trust these doctors at their word even when it felt so incredibly strange and uncomfortable. Never before had I filled out so much paperwork. I felt like I had signed my life and finances away. Then we had to watch hours of video to document and prove to the fertility place that we really understood what we were committing to and that we understood all of the risks we were taking. During each video, I either cried or sat comatose. I would pray to God, asking why Michael and I had to suffer like this? Why is it so easy for some people to just have children, like some of the parents of my students. It made me angry because, as a teacher for a decade, I had witnessed the neglect and selfishness of some parents and I knew in my heart our child would be so well cared-for.

Michael and I took breaks between disappointing fertility doctor appointments. We just didn't trust the several doctors we had already seen. Each doctor took months to get an appointment, transferring medical documents required time and follow-up calls, and each one, of course, cost money. So much money. These doctors are not cheap. We visited a total of eleven. We knew we needed to be one hundred percent comfortable with any doctor we were going to have on this journey. A silver-lining to all these visits was that my insurance covered anywhere from fifty to ninety percent of my visits, medicines, and appointments. We couldn't have done any of this without my insurance.

After years of visits to the different fertility doctors and failed IUI and IVF attempts, we had to face the fact that these doctors were right. If we wanted to have our beautiful baby, we would need to use a donor egg. For me, that was a truly emotional rollercoaster. I had to mourn that my baby would not look like me, have my genetics, or be biologically related to me. Then the first time we looked up the potential donors, I had no idea that their pictures were going to be the first thing I saw. My heart sunk into my stomach as thoughts of, "This is who my baby will look like," and "What if I see the biological mother in the future and she sees my baby and knows that's her baby," and "My baby will ask why he or she doesn't look like me," and family will say, "Your child looks like Michael but I don't see a resemblance to you." I tortured myself with these terrible thoughts. Again, Michael came to the rescue with kind words like, "Yes, but you will be growing our baby. Our baby will have some of you because you are making every part of that child. You will have a connection stronger than anything because our baby will be inside of your body. You are going to make the world's greatest mother. I love you."

It took me a full year to come to terms with the fact that I couldn't use my own eggs. It took that entire year to heal and accept and make peace with my reality. With each month that passed, anxiety of me and Michael getting older didn't fade. We watched younger friends, cousins, and family have child after child after child. At every party we attended, people would watch me to see if I was drinking. After years of anxiety over this, I finally said, "Fuck it. If they love me they won't be nosy." I had to let go of people's insensitivities because it really pissed me off for a very long time. NONE of this was easy to digest or accept.

I buried what was happening to us for years. I was alone and depressed. I went to a fertility appointment and as I sat there, I looked up and saw one of my friends. I stood up and sat next to her and said, "Hey." It was instant tears for us both. After our appointments that day, we spoke and made time to get together to basically cry and express all we had been through and how scary and lonely and terrifying this journey was. That was almost three years ago and it was the best thing that could have happened to me because it allowed me to see that others go through this, too. I finally began to open up to my amazingly supportive sisters and to my best friend. Michael felt relieved too because he finally saw my demeanor become a little more relaxed. He had begged me to talk to someone besides him, but it felt like it hurt too much to speak and that I would only cry if I opened my mouth. But he was right; talking felt like a little weight had been lifted and I wasn't so alone anymore.

In August of 2018, we had our first donor eggs transferred to our fertility place and anxiously awaited the news of how the embryos were progressing. The first call was great news. We had six viable embryos, but the next day, during a staff meeting, I got the call that all six embryos didn't make it. The laboratory staff was basically at a loss for words because this was extremely rare. I was devastated. I couldn't even go back to my meeting. I thought that after all this time, after a year of searching for the perfect donor, we had the right one, the perfect eggs that both my husband I agreed upon. But now we had nothing. Again. My first call was obviously to Michael. We shared in the heartbreak and anger. But then I had to call the donor bank that we were using and talk to them about this rare occurrence because we had purchased a

$40,000 reassurance plan. This expensive plan, not covered by insurance, guaranteed us six tries over the course of three years. I had to ensure that this wasn't going to count as one of our six tries because it was clear to me that this was an exception. Luckily, they confirmed that this would not count against us. So that night, Michael and I wasted NO time and selected another egg donor. We signed and sent in the paperwork within twenty-four hours of the loss of our six embryos. After all we had already been through, we knew the only way to move was forward.

Within this same time frame, the fertility doctor with whom we had been working changed offices. So now we had to change doctors again. This was frustrating because we had to wait to set up an appointment to meet the new doctor. Luckily, we liked this new doctor and felt comfortable with her.

More medicine, medicine, medicine. Shots, pills, and more shots. Over the course of the five and a half years of our journey, I could fill a tub with all of the different medications, shots, and needles that we used. From vaginal pills three times a day to painful intramuscular injections twice a day to patches as big as a jelly jar lid, it was painful and intense for both Michael and me. Each time an IVF or IUI round failed, we felt such a waste of time, energy, pain, and money.

It's not easy to just be ok when attempt after attempt has failed, not to mention the general risks of using these medicines for an extended period. Worrying was and is exhausting. Some days, going to work, going to family parties, or attending get-together with friends, I couldn't shake my anger or frustration or annoyance with what we were going through. Even though I could talk to people who truly cared for me, sometimes, it was just too much, and I wanted to be alone. But knowing I had people to turn to when I was ready to talk again was a saving grace.

. . .

Today am fighting a sour stomach, eating sliced almonds, and trying to choke down water, which I used to find refreshing. Why? Because on November 17th, Michael and I had our donor egg implanted inside of me. And on November 28th, we found out that WE ARE PREGNANT! After all these years, we are PREGNANT! The joy we have cannot truly be expressed. We have had two wonderful ultrasound appointments with our fertility doctor. We "graduated" from our fertility place this past week, and the best graduation gift ever is to know our baby's heartbeat is strong. We are eight weeks pregnant and are so excited to be able to tell our supportive and wonderful family and friends in just a few weeks. Sometimes it still feels surreal to know that we are pregnant, but then the sour stomach, bloating, and gas remind me that it's all true. I have to say it to believe it.

Our journey is not over and the past few years have been filled with a lot of pain. But what I couldn't see at the time was Michael and I were growing stronger as individuals and as a couple. I truly once thought no one could possibly know what I was going through, but that was not and will never be true. No matter what we were facing, someone else was facing it, too. We were never alone. And now that I'm pregnant, awaiting the birth of this baby and loving every minute of my pregnancy, I will truly never again be alone. And I couldn't be more grateful.

How Many Kids Do You Have

By Jenny Lamb

Selfish. That is what I told everyone when they asked why Jake and I hadn't started having children yet. And it was the truth. I enjoyed sleeping in, lazy weekends, nights out, and a reprieve from responsibility. As a teacher, I felt a tremendous amount of responsibility everyday for the students in my classroom, and allowing myself the time to breathe on the weekends and evenings was a necessity.

However, at the age of thirty two, we decided it was time. We were blissfully ignorant. In August 2012, we actually started "trying" for a baby. And let me tell you, when you flip that switch to *trying*, it is all-consuming. I never realized I wanted something more badly than when I continued to receive negative pregnancy results month after month. 2013 began and we were no closer to conceiving. I bought a fancy little machine that measured my ovulation hormones every morning. In 2013, I started each day by peeing on sticks. If I saw a smiley face, it was go time! This was fun for a couple of months, but when trying to make a baby turned into a chore, sex became mundane and even a burden. After months of stress and ovulation tests and sex-at-certain-times-only and a couple visits to the doctor to try and speed things up, we finally conceived our first child in May of 2013. I vividly remember sitting on the toilet, watching the pregnancy test turn positive and starting to shake. Initially, pre-pregnancy, I had grand plans to create a cute way of telling Jake, my husband, when we had finally conceived. All of those ideas dissolved when I saw that double line. I had to tell him immediately. Many family members and close friends had been on this journey with us and we told them immediately when we had the results. Excitement was an understatement; this was the first grandchild on both sides of the family. Everyone was elated.

I was extremely sick the entire pregnancy, but other than that, the baby and I were doing well. All of my sonograms, as well as my bloodwork, were normal. Jake and I knew we were having a boy, and after careful deliberation, we decided to name him Jackson Douglas Lamb. After having multiple baby showers and decorating the nursery, we couldn't have been more ready for this baby.

On January 18th, 2014, I was thirty-seven weeks and five days pregnant. Jake and I had breakfast with my mom and then we took a trip Target to add a few more baby essentials to the house before Jackson arrived. He could come at any time! We could be parents soon! Walking through Target, I anticipated the surprise of my water breaking and rushing to the hospital; it all seemed to be such an exciting experience. We shopped around a little more and spent a nice afternoon together. Jake later went to his friend's house while I stayed home for a quiet relaxing evening of Chinese food and guilty-pleasure television. Jake arrived back home around 9:30 that night. I was laying on the couch and started to think about how little I had felt Jackson move that day. He was breach so his movement was limited anyway. I drank some orange juice and grabbed a bag of frozen vegetables to put on my extremely large belly. Nothing. At this point, I knew something was wrong and I started freaking out. It was mother's intuition. My husband, on the other hand, was calm and cool, not really understanding what I wasn't feeling. He calmly told me to get dressed and we rushed to the hospital.

I was immediately rushed to the delivery floor where a heartbeat could not be found. The multiple nurses who came in tried to comfort me and tell me that perhaps they were not using the machine correctly. However, I knew he had passed. But these nurses refused to tell me until my doctor arrived. Of course, my doctor, who has since had his license revoked and is no longer practicing, was out of town, so another doctor had to come and tell me our baby, Jackson, was dead. I hated the doctor for this. I wanted to scream and tell her she smelled like the cigarette she had just smoked on her way to tell me about my dead baby. I wanted to run out of the room, run back home, eat the Chinese food as I had been doing before any of this became real.

Jake didn't believe her and had her point to the screen where the heart should be beating. I had to cover my eyes; it was horrifically awful to see this heart, the heart that I built, that should be beating, lie so still.

On top of this horrific news, the new doctor, with whom I had no relationship, wanted me to deliver naturally that night.

Had Jackson not been breech, this suggestion from the ashtray doctor may not have been so outlandish and hurtful. I knew delivering a breech baby was more difficult and selfishly, I did not want to endure a more physical pain when I was already suffering significant emotional pain. When I told the doctor he was breech and the delivery would be difficult, her exact words were, "but he is already gone." I was shocked and numbed by her words and felt pressure to succumb to "doctor's orders."

So she induced me and we waited. For hours I tried to sleep and I just wanted it all to be over; I wanted the bandage ripped off. When my doctor finally arrived the next morning, I had not dilated at all. Jake and I made the decision to have a C-section to put an end to this nightmare so we could begin grieving.

One of the things we thought would facilitate our healing process would be to get pregnant again and as fast as we could. My monthly cycle was taking a very long time to return due to stress and grief, but only after two months of trying, it worked. In May of 2014, we found out we were pregnant again. Our joy was short lived, however, when we miscarried a week later. To add salt to the wound, when my OB's office found out about the miscarriage, they looked at some results taken from my placenta and found that Jackson had a rare genetic disorder.

The doctors thought it would be in our best interest to seek genetic counseling to understand what may be going on with our babies.

Thank goodness the genetic counselors believed that Jackson's genetic syndrome was just bad luck and the miscarriage after even worse luck. I was happy to hear that news and continued to believe that we would someday be blessed with a healthy child. The months of disappointment continued and after more visits to the doctor, we were told we needed a little "help." And so the shots began. I needed shots in my stomach during the first part of my cycle and shots in my ass at the end of my cycle. I had a cyst on my ovary and the shots were supposed to help with that, as well as with conception. However, we were still not pregnant and although we were getting the "help" we needed, I was sadder and more devastated than ever.

The one-year anniversary of Jackson's death was approaching and, not pregnant yet, Jake and I were both in a terrible place. We decided to take a trip to San Diego to "get away." I was so excited to take this trip, to get away, and to drown my sorrows in alcohol, when we received the most unexpected news. As our plane landed in California, I got a call from the doctor's office telling me I was pregnant. My doctor's office knew from a blood test because they were checking all of my hormone levels every month. When I didn't get my period after thirty-four days, I assumed I was not pregnant again, and I got my blood drawn to know for certain what was going on inside my body.

Of course we were excited, but a huge part of me was actually pissed. I had planned on selfishly drinking and for once not thinking about the loss of my son. And now I couldn't. I also truly felt that the pregnancy would end in another loss and so what was the point of being excited, of decorating a nursery, of planning for daycare, of dreaming of holding a new baby, of anything. So this trip-to-forget ended up being a trip that focused on me being pregnant and therefore the losses we had previously suffered.

The entire pregnancy was horrible despite the fact that I had found a new doctor who was tremendous and empathetic. She used every resource available to her to reassure my nerves, but it was rough. My counselor helped me use breathing techniques to try and work through the stress, but as the pregnancy got further along and closer to the thirty-eight week mark (when we lost Jackson), I needed the baby out! I asked my doctor if we could deliver at thirty-seven weeks and four days to help ease my anxiety and sheer terror at potentially losing another child, and she agreed.

Nine months after that phone call in California, after so much fear and pain and doubt, I heard the cries of my LIVE baby. I have never heard a sweeter sound than Philip Jackson Lamb crying. I began crying in disbelief that he was here and healthy. I had a birth plan that immediately required the doctors to give Philip to me so I could hold him. My husband and I were just staring at this beautiful baby boy that we had waited for so long to love and nurture. Philip then immediately latched on to breastfeed, and the moment was perfect.

Prior to celebrating the birth of Philip, I made a very detailed birth plan to avoid any of the emotionally triggering questions that nurses might ask me. My requests, for the most part, were respected, but I had one nurse and a lactation consultant ask about my other birth and baby. It was gut-wrenching and thinking about the two babies I didn't get to hold, while holding my brand new Philip, was confusing; I was filled with grief. I remember looking at my sister and with one look, she knew what I needed. The lactation consultant was out of the room before I could count to ten.

Some women say that recovering from a C-section is extremely difficult. However, I had so much joy pumping through my veins that I was showering the next morning and ready to go home in less than twenty-four hours. The nurses kept telling me to send the baby to the nursery so Jake and I could sleep, but we wanted to watch Philip's every breath. That baby was not leaving our side.

Actually bringing a baby home from the hospital is a feeling that most parents take for granted but one that I will never forget. The ride home from the hospital after losing Jackson was the longest and quietest car ride of my life. Walking into the house with an empty nursery was excruciating. There is no greater devastation than losing a child, coming home to a quiet house after a C-section, closing the door to a nursery that wouldn't ever have a baby in it, looking at the gifts that would never be used, the boobs agonizingly full of milk, the car seat in the car, the six weeks off of work without a baby to care for, the marketing emails congratulating you on your baby. But when we finally got Philip home, I felt so glorious in motherhood that within the year we wanted to expand our family further.

Close to Philip's first birthday, we found out we were pregnant again. I remember celebrating and being so happy that we were already on the way to continuing our family. However, when I went in for my first sonogram appointment, Jake and I were met with disappointment once again. Because of the efforts it took for Jake and I to conceive, I knew exactly how pregnant I was: ten weeks. The sonographer asked me twice how far along I thought I was and could there be any mistake. We said no. "The baby is only measuring at five weeks. I am so sorry," she said. We were then whisked away to another room to talk with a midwife about the next steps. Since I had not physically expelled the baby yet, the midwife wanted to run some blood work over the next couple days for specific counts and levels to make sure it was a miscarriage. This took three horrific days. Once the bloodwork came back confirming that it was a miscarriage, I had the choice to wait until my body was able to eliminate on its own, or I could take some medication to speed the process.

I decided to give my body a week. However, after a few days of carrying another dead baby inside of me, I just wanted it to be over. So I took medication on Saturday night, after I organized, set up, and chaperoned the school's Homecoming dance, and hoped it would wait to start working until after all of the Homecoming decorations had been cleaned up on

Sunday. Because on top of all this, I was still a working teacher and student council advisor, with students, events, and responsibilities. I had to pretend everything was fine in front of hundreds of dancing, clueless students, who just wanted to have fun.

I started bleeding the next morning and actually felt relieved that another terrible nightmare was ending. However, the bleeding stopped and I took more medication, but nothing happened. I called the OB's office and my next step was a D&C. This process of the medication and the D&C took a week. I was incredibly sad and hurt when I returned to school and everyone thought I had taken an entire week off of school after Homecoming because the week was just "too much" for me. They had no idea what I was going through, but I did not tell anyone I worked with or any students why I was gone. I couldn't handle other people knowing.

After the D&C, my cycle came back relatively quickly, but I had brown bleeding and the doctors thought this could be a sign of uterine cancer. They wanted to check for this before we began trying again for another baby. It was an additional hurdle. But in May of 2017, we were pregnant again! One of my hormones (progesterone) was dangerously low throughout the pregnancy and therefore required shots two times a week in the ass. By the end of the pregnancy, there wasn't a spot on my butt that didn't have scar tissue. But after nine months of morning sickness and bi-weekly shots, Jake and I had our beautiful baby girl, Madigan Elizabeth.

I was much more relaxed about our hospital stay leading up to the scheduled delivery and did not have a birth plan for Madigan as I did for Philip's birth. We were more confident as parents after Philip, and much more relaxed after everything that we had been through together. When my daughter was delivered, the doctors took their time with her and that was more than difficult. I watched these large red numbers on a digital clock count up to over ten minutes before they set her on my chest. My fears of something being wrong were alleviated when she was finally with me, and I felt so thankful for this healthy girl. Jake and I also allowed Madigan to go to the nursery for at least two hours a night so we could get some sleep.

Throughout my process of motherhood, my social circle grew significantly smaller. After losing Jackson, I could not be around anyone. In fact, I did not return to teaching for sixteen weeks, knowing the students would have no understanding of what I had been through. I had numerous close friends who were pregnant, and seeing their large and growing bellies was a trigger. I needed time to figure out how to cope with the grief and loss while others found joy. I needed to figure out how to answer the question, "How many kids do you have?"

While I have found a new normal after losing a child and two pregnancies, my heart will always be strikingly different than it was before any of this happened. When people ask me how many children I have, I don't really know how to respond. But that is what motherhood has become for me. It is a sense of sadness and bad luck and devastation, as well as intense joy and love and unimaginable connection to my kids. And I move forward because I carry with me a stronger empathy and understanding of humanity. My first son was part of me and he still is. After I had him, I was reborn with a new connection to all the other mothers out there who have lost children and pregnancies and who are packing lunches and changing diapers and snuggling babies and bandaging knees no matter what has happened in their pasts.

My youngest child is now almost two years old. I feel blessed with my two children, but I still feel grief at the loss of my other son. I'm reminded of him constantly, and in reflection, I am proud that I have found the ability to move forward. I am happy with my life, but I don't think I will ever feel content. There are missing pieces. My happiness is a broken happiness, and that is simply my new normal.

Before and After

By Sarah Abete

I: Preface

Memory is a tricky thing. The mind can be kind and allow one to forget all the gory details of a terrible moment. Or it can hang on relentlessly, white-knuckled, to an episode one would rather forget. It is a glorious mystery why some memories are so ingrained, while others are hazy. From my personal experience, the memories that leave lasting impressions are often the most painful.

At this point in my life, I have birthed five beautiful, healthy, and exquisite daughters via Cesarean section. Each birth has been unique in its own right. However, when my daughters ask me to retell the details of their birth, the specifics become so muddled that I cannot differentiate one birth from another. The only memories I do have tend to be happy. Perhaps this is my mind's self-preservation, my fragile brain's way of saying, "It wasn't so bad! You did great!"

Yet, my daughters are relentless in their pursuit for information about their births. They want to know details about what it was like for me and their daddy to see them for the first

203

BIRTHMARKS

time, what my first impressions were, what they looked like, and what I thought. For one daughter, my third and smallest baby, I can only smile when I remember feeling her squishy leg and commenting on how warm she was while I lay cruciform on the operating table. Her warmth stuck with me the most. That and her baldness: as bald as a cueball! She was perfect.

Another daughter, my first child and most exciting delivery to date, was born six weeks prematurely. She made quite a grand and bold entrance into the world and shocked us all by being a petite little girl weighing only four pounds and twelve ounces (I just knew that I was going to have a nine pound baby boy!), by arriving before her baby shower, and by refusing to wait for her father to arrive in the operating room. She was a girl on a mission to get her life started early. She remains my most punctual child and absolutely abhors being late. She, too, was perfect.

Another daughter's birth is emblazoned in my memory by two small birthmarks: one on the back of her head and one on her upper shoulder. The birthmarks were raised and red and to me they were a small touchstone. A simple reminder each time I touched her that this baby was mine. No mistaking her for other babies, even when the lights were out. Another perfect baby.

And then there are vague memories attached to my youngest daughter's birth. Considering that she was born the most recently it would make sense that I would have the most clear memories of her birth. And yet again, only the trivial details emerge: the kind and gregarious anesthesiologist who patiently talked me through my irrational fears of having a spinal block rather than an epidural, my sweet baby latching on for the first time, and finally bringing the little nugget home from the hospital to meet her gaggle of doting, older sisters. Perfection embodied.

Other small details make up the deliveries of my daughters. Mostly, when I remember their birth stories, I am filled with such awe and gratitude for their little lives that I can hardly contain myself. Thankfully, if the need arises for more details, I can rely on the memories of my husband and friends to remind me of their unique birthdays.

There is one birth, however, that is set apart from the rest of my five daughters. It is set apart precisely because I remember every single detail. There is no foggy memory here; no hazy confusion about what her birth entailed. Her birth is etched in my mind like a branding. And as I type this now, nearly eleven years later, I can recount every detail as if it just happened. My second daughter left a mark then and continues to leave a mark now. This is her birth story. This is the story of my feisty, courageous, bold, and loud daughter. The one who taught me to heal and hope.

II: Before

For some women, they describe it like being hit by a truck. For others, they call it a deep, dark pit with no way out. Still other women describe it as pure hell: sadness, despair, and loneliness. One woman described it as a heavy and suffocating blanket. For me, it was like being run over by a train. An enormous, seemingly never-ending black steam engine.

For weeks before the birth of my second daughter, Annalise, I could hear the steam engine coming. I was unsettled, anxious, tearful, and frightened, yet the exact reason for my uneasiness evaded me. I could not put my finger on what was going on inside of me. I blamed hormones, lack of sleep, and fear of having another preterm delivery (my first baby having been born prematurely due to a painless, bloodless placenta abruption). Ironically, my first's birth proved to be more joyful and exciting than the birth I was weeks from experiencing with my second child.

I could feel the rumblings of the steam engine as it headed toward the station. I could hear the percussive and incessant warning long before it reached its destination. The train was barrelling down the track toward me. I knew it was coming. I could hear it, feel it, and even spied the dark grey steam billowing over the horizon. I am sad to say that I did not know what these warnings meant. But I knew three things most definitely: I was scared, I was lonely, and I would surely be locked up in the mental ward very soon.

Out of fear, I couldn't express the terrifying thoughts that flooded me. I thought it better to keep everything to myself. I refused to tell anyone, and I cried a lot. These thoughts plagued me. They would not let up, even when I slept (which I rarely did). I had thoughts of jumping out of windows, jumping in front of trains, hurting myself, and hurting my loved ones. I was scared of myself, scared of my house, scared of my car, and scared to be alone.

The symptoms that I had before and after the birth of my second daughter were, what a psychologist would later tell me, "textbook symptoms of postpartum depression." Every single one was there: the terrifying thoughts, the insomnia, fear, anxiety, crying fits, delusional thinking, and fear of being alone. I isolated myself prior to my daughter being born and pleaded with God to take the thoughts away. Because of my fear, unstable mind, and raging pregnancy hormones, I told no one about the torment I was experiencing. Little did I know that the black steam engine I had heard all through my pregnancy would roar into the station right after birth and I would be plunged into a state of depression that I thought would surely end my life. The fear and intrusive thoughts that began before the birth of my second daughter escalated exponentially once she was born.

III: During

When the postpartum train finally ran me over, my life was sorted into two categories: Before Annalise (BA) and After Annalise (AA). The day of my second child's birth was filled with no excitement, anticipation, or eager expectation to hold my precious baby. Since my first baby was born prematurely and suffered no complications at birth or after, I was convinced that my second baby would have all the complications that my first avoided. I was plagued by the anxious thought that the baby growing in my womb would not make it to her birth alive. I knew that the painless, bloodless abruption that had caused the preterm birth of my first baby was highly unlikely to occur again. However, I also knew that many placenta abruptions do not have the same happy endings that I was given.

Days before my scheduled C-section, I was still resistant to allow myself to imagine holding my baby or changing her tiny diaper. I hadn't even washed the baby clothes or packed a bag for the hospital. I just knew that my baby would die. It was a thought on which I had perseverated for the entire pregnancy.

When my sweet second was born, I couldn't focus. My thoughts were wild and irrational, dark and scary. The surgery was successful, but the circumstances surrounding it still make my skin crawl.

On the evening of December 11, I had a routine OB check that preceded my daughter's scheduled birth by one short day. At this appointment, my doctor discovered that my blood pressure was slightly elevated and determined that, rather than waiting for my C-section on the following morning, he preferred that I drive to the hospital to deliver that evening.

When we arrived at the hospital, I continued to feel "not quite right." I was not excited to meet my baby. I still felt the doom hanging over my head that she would die within my womb.

The dark and terrifying black thoughts that had plagued me for months were intensifying. I was anxious, flustered, distracted, and jittery.

Once we were checked in, my husband arrived and put on a gown. He smiled and joked when his surgical pants ripped and asked the nurse for a larger pair. I did not crack a smile. How could he be smiling and jovial at a time like this? Then the nurses began preparing me for surgery. I was a mess inwardly. I held onto the hope that, "Once I see my baby, all will be well. I just need to see her, touch her, hold her, and smell her. Then I will feel so much relief."

The nurse walked me into the operating room while the surgeons were scrubbing in and the attending physician was putting on her gown and surgical gear. Anesthesia was administered, I was laid back cruciform and the surgery commenced. "Focus on the baby, Sarah. Soon this will all be over and you will meet your baby," I thought. I hung on to the hope that meeting my daughter would squelch the dark thoughts. I put my faith into the doctors' very capable hands. With my husband by my side, I watched the surgeons hang the sheet that separates the head of the patient from her abdomen.

To my disappointment and disgust, the surgeons turned the birth of my baby into what may well have been a routine appendectomy. My doctor and the attending physician paid little attention to me on the other side of the curtain. I felt like I was just a body. Conversations of holiday plans, questions about one's children and other sorts of chitchat ensued while my baby was removed from my womb.

When she was born, a brief "baby girl" was muttered by one of the physicians and she was whisked away by a nurse. As the nurse was leaving the OR with my precious child, she flashed me a brief glimpse of my baby's face. I was allowed only a momentary glance of Annalise peeping out of a receiving blanket, only a second or two to note that she had a headful of dark, fuzzy hair before the nurse rushed out of the room with her. I was allowed no smell, no touch. No staring into the dark brown eyes of this new person. Not even a moment to kiss her chubby cheeks. I needed to touch her skin. I needed to smell her fuzzy head. I remember thinking, "That's it? That's all I get? I can hardly see her from here! She's forty feet away! Where is she going! I need her! A moment ago, she was punching me in my ribs and now she's gone!" Numbness and emptiness filled me where a baby had just been.

Unfortunately, I did not advocate for my needs at all. I was insecure and distrustful of my feelings and I was also worried that the doctors might sense my neediness and impending nervous breakdown and take my daughter away from me. Instead, I allowed huge, hot, silent tears to slide down my cheeks as I tried to smile and act normal. On the outside, I may have looked calm and collected, but I was truly a disaster. My hell on earth was just beginning.

IV: After

The vital moments of bonding with my baby immediately after her birth were stolen from me. They were ripped out of me and whisked away down the hall under the pretence of "hospital protocol." I believe that if I had been able to bond with baby early on, I may have experienced less postpartum depression (PPD). However, the PPD train was already in motion and it, combined with my terrible birth experience, would not relent for a very long time.

When the surgery was complete, after all my organs were properly placed back into my abdomen, and I was glued shut (yes, glued), I was wheeled into a recovery room, which still haunts me. In this bright and sterile hospital room, I was graciously handed the remote control to a television and then left completely alone. On a small and staticky television, old reruns of *Friends* were playing. To this day, I cannot watch *Friends* without having terrible flashbacks.

In the hospital bed, I laid there alternately looking at the oozing incision in my stomach and the sitcom on the television. "What in the hell has just happened? Where is my baby? Why am I all alone?" More big, hot tears ran down my face.

After what seemed like hours, my mother and husband arrived to check on me and to show me blurry Polaroid pictures of Annalise taken by the nurses in the nursery. "She's beautiful, Sarah! Wait till you see her!" gushed my mom. "Look! The nurses gave her a bath and put her hair in a Mohawk! She has so much hair!" reported my husband. As they showed me pictures of her and reported the news that the nurses had given her a bottle "because she was fussy and they wanted to soothe her," I attempted to comprehend all the information. My husband handed me a blurry Polaroid of Annalise in her bassinet and a blue cardstock piece of paper with her footprints on it for me to keep. He kissed my head, told me how proud he was of me, promised to come check on me again shortly, and left me to peek in on our baby, my mom following.

My head was spinning after they left. The nurses gave Annalise her first bath and gave her a bottle without me? She was given formula without my consent? Repeatedly, I had expressed my desire to exclusively breastfeed my baby. Why was I, the mother, so left out of these early decisions? More tears, more stuffing down of sad feelings, and more isolation.

After ninety minutes in recovery, I was finally brought up to my hospital room. I was eager to hold my baby, to smell her, to touch her. "It won't be long now!" I thought. I was wrong.

From the time of her delivery to the time when Annalise was finally placed in my arms, three and a half long hours had passed. This still makes me weep. I needed her. She needed me. And yet, we were kept apart for no significant reason. I was healthy and so was she. I know that many mothers are forced to spend hours and days apart from their baby right after birth. And this breaks my heart. For reasons out of their control (heart surgery, trouble breathing, prematurity, etc.), babies are removed from their mother's care and placed in a safe and controlled neonatal intensive care unit with brilliant nurses and caring doctors to attend to them. My first daughter spent time in the NICU and I appreciate the care and expertise of the NICU health care professionals. There are perfectly justifiable reasons for a baby to be separated from her mother; however, there was no reason for Annalise to be separated from me. This was the unfortunate and devastating protocol of the hospital.

I wish I could say that once I finally held Annalise in my arms, all of my anxiety finally abated and I fell madly in love with my daughter. I wanted to; I desperately and fiercely desired to love her. But I didn't. I felt nothing but fear, terror and isolation. How could a mother feel nothing for her newborn baby girl? What was wrong with me?

Later that night, the terror continued. All of my family left me so that I could "get some rest" and the intrusive thoughts escalated. I began to sob uncontrollably and called for a nurse to help me. She scoffed at me and said, "Why are you crying? Haven't you done this before? Isn't this your second baby?" This woman.

Oh how I wish this nurse had taken the time to ask me some real questions and had contacted a mental health professional for help. Perhaps my healing would have begun that day. But it did not. I did not sleep that night and continued to cry. I prayed that God would take all my scary thoughts away.

On the following morning, visitors began to arrive with gifts and well wishes. Again, on the outside I appeared happy, but the demon was still lurking. Specifically, I remember two friends coming up to the hospital to visit me. One of the friends, a sweet teacher with whom I had recently become very close, brought a gift for the new baby: a yellow, zip-up winter onesie. It was the kind of outfit that a mother would dress her baby in when she was planning to take her out for a walk on a cold day; it was fleeced lined, very warm and had a hood attached to it. Instantly, a terrifying image of my daughter wearing the winter garment filled my mind. I imagined zipping up the coat too tightly and she suffocated. The baby was blue. When this image popped into my mind, I panicked and began to sweat but said nothing to my friends. Hallucinations like these plagued me day and night. I was scared to be alone. But I was more scared to tell anyone about these terrible thoughts. Surely, someone would come and take away my daughters. Surely, I was an unfit mother.

After the appropriate amount of time for small talk, my friends put on their coats and said their goodbyes. Oh, how I did not want them to go! To be left alone with the baby, with my dark thoughts, and with the scary yellow jumpsuit was more than I could bear. Yet I said nothing. I hugged them both and promised to call if I needed anything. But how could I possibly tell them what I was really thinking? I was so scared that if I told them what was really happening, they would report me to DCFS and my babies would be removed from my custody.

Later on that second day in the hospital, my catheter was removed and I was encouraged to get up and walk around my hospital room. My first thought was that a shower would help to calm my mind. The warm shower felt nice but did not help with my mental state. As I stepped carefully out of the shower, I saw a hook on the back of the bathroom door. Instantly, a hallucination of my baby hanging there filled my mind. I gasped out loud and felt my knees buckle. I nearly fell to the ground. What was wrong with me? Why was I having these thoughts? I sobbed as I toweled off and gingerly dressed into a new hospital gown. All I knew was that I did NOT want to be alone.

When I was discharged from the hospital, more terrifying thoughts followed me around my cozy little home. Even routine chores sent me into a state of panic. Bath time was excruciatingly painful (hallucinations of the baby drowning or of me dropping the slippery little infant), making dinner seemed like a scene from a horror movie (delusions of me cutting the baby while I chopped vegetables) and even breastfeeding Annalise brought me no comfort (visions of me suffocating her with my engorged breast).

The intrusive thoughts that battered my mind came fast and furious. I felt like I was being pelted with invisible bullets. I had no intention of harming my child. These thoughts were not mine; they were symptoms of my illness. But they were constant.

Days and days of crying, sleepless nights, and not eating caught up with me. I was a mess. At my one week check up in my OB's office, I weighed less than I had prior to getting pregnant. I had lost over thirty pounds in one week. I was visibly distraught. Finally, I broke down and told my mom what was happening. I told her about the scary thoughts and I wept and wept. She did her best to help me, but she had no experience with PPD. All she knew was that I needed help and that she was going to make sure I got it. She asked me to call my doctor and explain what was happening. To my disappointment, my doctor let me down. He downplayed my symptoms, told me that I needed to get some rest and that I was too hard on myself. Reluctantly, he prescribed me some antidepressants and told me to start seeing a therapist.

The therapist that I found was terribly unequipped to handle the severity of my depression. She had no prior experience with PPD and she was very young. The intrusive thoughts that I shared with her left her puzzled and perplexed. She didn't understand why I was having thoughts of harming my baby because she did not understand how PPD works on the mind of a new mother. I felt like a monster. The only solace she provided for me was the clear diagnosis of PPD and the knowledge that PPD is temporary. She told me that I would eventually get better.

Once I finally had a diagnosis, I set about like a detective to learn anything and everything that I could about PPD. I read blogs, books, and articles. The librarians knew me by name as I weekly checked out books about PPD. I met authors and contacted women who had overcome PPD. After months and months of researching, digging deep, and praying hard, I finally started to find answers. The dark thoughts were still present, but I had learned some strategies to deal with them.

One of the most profound insights happened at a doctor's appointment nearly two years after Annalise was born, when I was still dealing with some PPD. I was put in contact with a kind and humble psychiatrist at a South Chicago doctor's office. During my first appointment, I shared everything. I cried as I told him of my deep desire to have more children. I cried as I mourned the months of depression that I experienced after Annalise's birth. I cried as I told him about the misinformation and stigma that abounds in our culture about PPD. This doctor, Dr. G, patiently listened to all of my lamentations. And then he looked at me and softly said, "If you want to grow your family, we will be here to help you do that. Postpartum depression is a temporary and very treatable condition. If you want more children, go ahead and have them and we will help you through all of it."

Slowly, I was able to heal, daily chores did not bring me terror, and I could allow the bad thoughts to roll off of me. The healing process was slow, but it was finally happening.

The symptoms that I experienced were very severe. In fact, my kind psychologist, Dr. G., suggested that perhaps if I had received the proper treatment and diagnosis immediately after Annalise's birth, I may have avoided the months and months of agony. He told me the scary thoughts are a symptom of post-partum depression obsessive compulsive disorder (PPD-OCD). The obsessive thoughts that flashed into my mind were a symp-tom of my greatest fear: my baby dying. And these fears, when tainted with the disease of PPD-OCD, played out in my mind as ME being the one harming my daughter. These symptoms of the illness seemed to make no sense, but once some light was shed on them, I was able to hold them at a distance and not give them as much control.

The knowledge that I gained from my research, combined with the support I received from Dr. G, my family, and close friends, emboldened me to remain open to the desire to have more chil-dren. (Little did I know that at my first appointment with Dr. G., I was already pregnant with my third daughter!)

Armed with the knowledge that I was pregnant for the third time and determined to have a completely different experience, I launched a "Find a New and Empathetic OB" campaign. I researched doctors. I asked friends for advice. And I found the kindest and most compassionate OB on the Southside of Chica-go, Dr. Mac. At our very first appointment, I felt at ease. I ex-plained everything. I laid my history out on the table. I detailed my first daughter's premature birth. I described my dissatisfaction with my second daughter's birth complete with my abhorrence for chitchat during surgery and my deep-seated desire to bond with my baby after birth. He listened. God bless the man, he really listened. And then he told me something that astounded me. He asked me if I would like to be his first patient for which he performed a "gentle C-section." Dr. Mac explained that he would like to do things differently. He would like mothers to see, touch, kiss, and even nurse their babies right there on the operating table. He believed firmly that it is in the best interest of both mother and baby to stay in close physical contact with each other. I was overjoyed! I wanted to kiss him! I felt like I had come full circle. My suffering was redeemed.

In addition, he informed me that he would need to change my antidepressant medication from Lexapro to Zoloft. Zoloft, he told me, was safer for pregnant women. I was very hesitant to switch antidepressants, but I decided to trust my new doctor and follow his lead. And thankfully, within four weeks, the anxiety that I had experienced for the past two years was lifted. Miracles were happening. And this was just the beginning.

Not only did Dr. Mac deliver my third baby using the "gentle C-section" technique, he went on to deliver my fourth and fifth babies, as well. He also implemented the "gentle C-section" technique as his protocol for all future Cesarean sections. And he was true to his word to me. I was able to hold, touch, kiss, and nurse my babies immediately. My bond with each of these babies was so intense, and so instant, and I am overwhelmed with gratitude for the amazing, compassionate and kind doctors like Dr. Mac and Dr. G.

I experienced PPD after the births of my subsequent children to varying degrees. But I was armed. I was prepared. Nonetheless, the looming monster still terrified me. Before each birth, I shuddered and tearfully told my husband, "I can't go through the hell of PPD again. I can't do it. What if I get locked up in the mental ward? I can't do it." And each time he confidently and calmly reminded me that I could do it because I had done it. I had overcome it. I had defeated the beast. And I was not alone.

V: Epilogue

I would be remiss if I did not add an addendum to my story of Annalise's birth with the update on where our relationship stands today, nearly eleven years later. I can happily say that by the time Annalise was six months old, she and I had developed an intense bond. Although our bond was delayed and took place later than I would have liked, she and I are as thick as thieves. The love I have for her is fierce. She is responsible for bringing out in me the most ferocious emotion possible: the love of someone who was hanging on for dear life and who would do anything to heal. Annalise taught me the valuable lesson that love is not a feeling; it is a choice and an action. Because even in my confused and sick state, I continued to choose to love her, to take care of her, and to believe that healing was possible.

For me, the most effective way to negate the terrible PPD thoughts and remove their power was to talk about them. I am so blessed and fortunate to have friends with whom I can be real, raw, and honest. My best friend and sister was able to laugh with me when I told her about the crazy thoughts I had after my fifth baby was born. "That's some craziness, Sarah! You sound like you are tripping on acid." Truth! Another friend called me every single day for two years after Annalise was born. She lived out of state and took it upon herself to check in on me. Yet another friend sent along a lifesaving NPR podcast that offered immense clarity on the origins of intrusive thoughts associated with OCD. How could I ever express my gratitude for this sort of love and devotion? When we, as mothers, bravely share our struggles and stick together, we are able to tackle huge and heavy monsters.

Very recently, I have been reflecting on the reason for my suffering. I know without a shadow of a doubt that my suffering has meaning and I know that good can come from it. Why did all this happen? To soften me, to keep my heart tender, to strengthen my faith, to humble me and to teach me my own strength. To teach me how to love myself and to love others. But mostly, I think this happened to me so that I could give hope to others, so that other women may not despair and feel abandoned and may not feel that they must go through it alone. When I was going through the throes of this illness, I wanted nothing more than for the thoughts to go away. I prayed and prayed and begged God to bring me back to "normal." But, if the pain had suddenly vanished, I would not have grown and learned all that I have. I would not have deepened my faith and felt God's presence in the most intimate of ways. I would have nothing to offer other women who suffer as I did. And I like to think that PPD has made me a better person.

It has not jaded me. I am not mad at God. I trust Him more. My faith has deepened. My heart is more open, and I know that I can get through really hard and scary things, and that I am not abandoned.

In the deepest part of my heart, I feel that my suffering has meaning because of my children. It is likely that one of my children will go through something hard and scary. If they will allow me to share my experiences, if they will be open to digging deep and learning, if they will reach out for help, they will find the same hope that I found. And they will not be alone.

The Crazy Mom

By Monica Falk

In my junior year of college, I received an unexpected email from one of my professors. He was looking for a student to babysit his two children on Wednesday mornings. Sitting in my cheap apartment, reading the line, "You seem like you'd be great with children," while tossing back some Tums for my hangover, I quickly replied with, "Count me in!" After sending, I remembered a snippet of information that was rather important: I didn't like children. But, always the people-pleaser, I decided to fake it 'til I made it.

About fifteen minutes into my first day of faking, I confirmed my hypothesis that children are exhausting. My professor had two sons; one was six months and the other three years. The sailing was anything but smooth. As I broke into a sweat trying to throw together a lunch for the toddler with the baby squawking in my arms, I happened to glance out the kitchen window. My professor's wife was in the backyard. She was seated in a lawn chair staring absently at their garden. If I was babysitting, why was their mother at home? Surely she had something else to do if they were paying for someone to watch their children.

As I cleaned up lunch, I glanced back out and saw that she was still there. Like a statue, she looked blankly ahead without any hint of movement. I babysat a few more times before throwing in the towel. Each time, the children's mother sat, sometimes outside in the chair, sometimes in silence upstairs. I was frustrated on the days that she stayed inside. Her three-year-old would stand at the gate at the bottom of the stairs and yell for his mommy. She would never come. She silently existed on the property like a ghost. I was frustrated that caring for her children wasn't easy, and it was even more difficult when her son knew she was home. On several occasions, I made jokes about her with my roommates, so much so that she became known as "the recluse" and "the crazy mom." Now, however, I wish I could revisit that woman. Because now I know her very well.

Pregnancy came with expectations. I knew children were exhausting, but I heard that they were worth the challenges. I expected sleepless nights, spit up on my shirt, cracked nipples, and a transition to complete selflessness. These are the Motherhood Rites of Passage. I didn't expect it to be easy, but I also didn't expect the most heartbreaking season of my life. Postpartum depression was not something I anticipated or really knew anything about. It hit me hard after the birth of my daughter, but it nearly took me out completely after the recent birth of my son. After the horrific struggles following the birth of my daughter, I convinced myself that one bout of depression was enough. The universe saw me struggle so deeply after having my first child that it would have mercy on me the second time. It would have to. I could not handle what I went through again.

How naive I was. Instead, with my second birth, this demon found its way back to me more quickly and much more intensely.

The first few days at home with my son fueled the Depression's ability to dig deep and take root. At one week postpartum, I stopped eating and showering. The hopefulness I held for nine months was completely and immediately suffocated by disabling sadness. I recalled reading that PPD typically increases in severity with each pregnancy, but I expected to do better the second time. I obsessively searched for ways that other women coped with postpartum disorders and refused to believe that I could possibly struggle as much as I did the first time. I was prepared this time. I knew what to look for. I had support. I could control my way out of this.

At four weeks postpartum, I stood in my bathroom holding a packet of sleeping pills while the rest of my house was asleep. By this point, I had already doubled the dosage of antidepressants that I had taken during my first round of PPD. I was ashamed of this. I knew that SSRI medications could take weeks to reach full effectiveness, but I didn't think I could make it much longer. As I stood there, my letter in my hand, figuring out how many pills it would take, with my perfect children sleeping peacefully across the hall, I realized how sorry I was. I was sorry that they had the misfortune to be given to such an unstable mother. I was sorry that I couldn't figure out how to stop crying in front of them. I was sorry that I wasn't strong enough to be who I wanted to be for them. I was sorry I was not enough. If I took these pills, I could give my children opportunities. They would be happy without my darkness dooming our home. My husband could remarry a steadfast woman and my babies could start over with a new mother, a better mother. They were young enough to forget about me. As I choked sobs and weighed my options, I felt a strong and sudden push to wake up my husband. I woke him with sobs against his chest, and I told him the truth about my plans.

In the weeks that followed, I had limitless support. My husband reached out to my parents and my in-laws, who literally saved my life. They sacrificed their time to keep me company and give me rest, watching my children while I tried to heal. These people repeatedly reminded me of my worth and helped our family function. My heart is raw and my early postpartum memories are forever tainted, but I am still here thanks to these people.

Having PPD does not mean that a mother doesn't love her children. Many times, people who have not experienced this horror believe that PPD automatically comes with detachment and disinterest. In both of my experiences, I felt incredible love for my children. This love both nurtured me and also ruined me. I drifted between obsessive protectiveness and utter self-hatred. I would try so hard to get my restless son to sleep, but then stay awake all night and stare at his chest to ensure that he was breathing. If I cried in front of my daughter, I would set a goal to hold it together for a few hours so I didn't stain her childhood memories. Many of my fears were irrational, but I loved my children so much that I kept overcompensating.

Looking back, most of the thoughts I had about my abilities were misplaced. I never once walked away or failed to provide for my children. And not one day did I neglect to tell them that I loved them. My love for them was infinite, too much almost, and I was unable to see that they were thriving, that they would be thriving, and that I was the reason.

Postpartum depression almost took away my children's mother and I am not sure the guilt I feel will ever subside. The letter I almost left for my children haunts me. But after two progressively more severe instances of postpartum depression, I know what mothers need, because it is what saved me. Postpartum mothers need tangible support beyond the simplistic questions on the Edinburgh Postnatal Depression Scale, haphazardly distributed at a six-week checkup. This support needs to be a community bound to you and your family, dedicated to helping you survive. I was lucky enough to have this community, but had I not, this essay would not exist.

My son is almost one now and though this has been a long recovery, I am feeling better. I have more clarity about everything I've been through. And with this clarity, I often reflect on my professor's wife. That poor, unmoving woman, staring into nothing, just trying to survive. With my new perspective, I feel ashamed of my previous judgment of her. I wish I could tell her now that I understand. That she is doing the best she can and that is good enough for the moment. I would tell her that her pain is real but the darkness is temporary. That people will help you if you let them. I would tell her that her children love her and will continue to love her, that she is and will always be enough. I would tell her that she needs a community to get her and her family through this, and that I am willing to be that community for her. I was that woman and I want her to know that she and any other woman going through this are not alone.

Broken

By Brooke Nelson

I walked into the doctor's office crying. The receptionist met me with the uncomfortable pity-eyes I had come to know well.

I stripped down, dragged the gown across my heaving chest. The nurse happily walked in with a baby blanket someone at the office had made for my new son. She proudly presented it to me and then placed it on the pillow before awkwardly patting my back and leaving. My doctor popped in, ready to release me after the six-week check, and instead found a crumpled, half-naked woman, rife with exhaustion and crushed hope. The postpartum depression questionnaire was a joke. He immediately hugged me. I had no pants on. This mattered none. It must be bad when a seasoned OB/GYN hugs a patient without pants on and neither of them really notices or cares. He prescribed Prozac, took my shoulders, and told me sternly, "You are a good mother. Don't you let anyone tell you otherwise. You are doing the best job you can. You don't deserve this." At the time, I couldn't believe him or stop crying. Now, I see that as such a kind gesture. One I desperately needed to heed, but couldn't.

I am a winner. I almost always win. And if I don't win, I try again until I do. I'm a leader, a do-er, and a decider. I know what I want, I do what I want, and I get what I want. So, with the birth of my first child, I was determined to do everything the way I wanted. I read the books. I had a doula. I took the hippie birthing class. I bought nursing shirts and nursing pillows and nipple balm. I was going to have the crap out of this baby. And I did. A thirty-hour labor without an epidural, and I had a healthy daughter. It was rough and painful and terrible. But I was the rare patient who refused all interventions. I didn't scream. I got her out with sheer grit and will. THE RIGHT WAY. And everything was great. I nursed her successfully in the hospital and everyone praised my job so far. Nurses clapped when I left the birthing room, my arms full of healthy baby. Of course I was good at this. I'm good at everything.

Except that I wasn't. After a week of nursing pretty much constantly, my daughter was losing weight. Oh my god. I couldn't keep my baby alive with my body. I didn't know this was a thing. No one said this could happen at the baby class. Nothing about this in the baby books. Boobs were for food. They knew what to do. This was supposed to be natural and easy.

This was the right way. The ONLY WAY. Ohmygod. Spinning. Internet nonstop. Message boards. All the advice. Teat Nazis. Lactation consultants. Teas. Oatmeal. SNS. Pumping and nursing and pumping and nursing. Tubes and machines. Crying and pumping and nursing and babies and mothers and sadness and despair.

I whipped my boobs out anywhere and everywhere. I pumped all day and all night, in the most literal sense. Still, not enough. Nipple blisters, plugged ducts, crying baby. Crying momma. My body sucks. My baby can't rely on just me. She would die if it were just us. Die. Die. Die. Formula. Depression. Failure.

With the surprising second pregnancy, after the shock, I saw my second chance. I could redo this whole thing. I hadn't planned on this but it could be good. My first pregnancy was difficult because of medical issues and high risk problems and a misdiagnosed fetal brain disorder for my daughter and a dangerous postpartum hemorrhage. But now I could have a nice pregnancy and a nice childbirth and a nice postpartum. I got a shrink and immediately started making plans to have all that I couldn't with the first. I had some complications during my second pregnancy, but overall, I was much more prepared for this pregnancy and birth and breastfeeding and postpartum. I wasn't happy or comfortable or ready. But I felt confident. I made mistakes the first time, but I could correct them now! Always the good student, I was excited to get a better grade. Especially with breastfeeding. This was what I was most looking forward to. I couldn't feed my first the way I wanted, but I was smarter now. I could do this the right way. I would nurse this baby until his first day of college! It would work this time! I would breastfeed constantly. Pump after every feed. Eat all the oatmeal. Lactation consultants on speed-dial. Wear loose shirts. Not sleep on my stomach. Skin-to-skin. Sleep with the baby. Massage breasts. Warm compresses. Hospital-grade pump. I WILL BREASTFEED THIS BABY AND I WILL BE THE BEST AT IT.

Except that I wasn't. After a painful but quick natural childbirth, and a wonderful "golden hour" with my new boy, he latched on and ate for two hours. I was elated. I did everything right and now I could reap the rewards. I was looking forward to a winter of snuggling and nursing and beginning our new family life. But after only three days on earth, my son wasn't peeing. Nursing constantly didn't work. He wasn't getting milk.

My boobs weren't working. Again. Formula in worried desperation at 11:00pm on his day three. Ohmygodifailedagainandsoonerthistime. Iamaterriblemother. Broken.

The depression was heavier and deeper this time. I had allowed myself to feel excited about this. Confident, even. I thought I would do a better job with all of my experience. And when that didn't happen, I sank. I woke up weeping in the middle of what little sleep I was getting. Among midnight sobs in a darkened room, I repeatedly told my husband I wanted to die. He would hold me, try to calm me, talk sense into me. "Our daughter is perfectly fine, smart, healthy, and she had formula. You had the same problems with her and everything is great. Look at her. She's good. It's ok." But that doesn't work on the postpartum brain, housed in the exhausted shirtless woman, wearing a nursing pillow, cradling her crying, hungry baby, trying so hard to make a body do what it won't. There was a goal, one way to it, and I couldn't get there. I was broken. I stopped living. I didn't leave the house for months. I only allowed one friend to visit, with the warning that I would be pumping or nursing pretty much the whole time. I permitted family over, but hesitantly, and really only because they insisted.

We had planned on fun Christmas adventures with our new four. But none of it would happen. I would punish my body for failing me yet again. I nursed every feeding for as long as my son would, usually an hour, then I would pump for twenty minutes, then feed breast milk and formula after. So, every hour I was either nursing or pumping or feeding. Around the clock. I was making most of his milk, but still not enough to keep him alive. I was sleeping maybe two hours a day, sometimes sitting in a chair between pumping sessions. My mom was worried: didn't leave my side. My husband was exhausted: this again. My daughter was confused and lonely. But I couldn't quit. Even the thought of stopping would throw me into a tailspin of desperation. He doesn't need me. This formula is stupid juice. He'll get cancer. ADHD. Never get into college. No jobs. It's all my fault. I'm a failure. A terrible mother. Twice.

On top of all of this, I desperately needed treatment for two autoimmune liver diseases that flared after childbirth, and my son developed an allergy to cow's milk that caused him to refuse to eat, poop blood, and scream all day and night. I had already made the commitment to avoid treatment for my liver until after nursing, since the medications were not compatible; this was my (stupid) level of dedication. I was willing to sacrifice some years of my life for this, no hesitation. And the fact that my son couldn't tolerate formula made this even worse. If only I could have been enough. If only I were enough for my children.

Once, during one of many middle-of-the-night fights between me and my poor, exhausted husband, he slammed a door and I burst into sobs. "I'm hanging on by a thread," I screamed. And he knew it. But he was hanging on by that same thread, we are heavy people, and the thread was thin and fraying. This breast-feeding thing was going to destroy my marriage. I didn't care.

My momma-friends would complain about their full boobs, talk about how much milk they were making. Some of them, literally gallons. They had no problems nursing. They had the baby, of-fered breast milk, and the boobs did their job. Nature worked as it should. I listened to a podcast about a woman who had breast cancer and breast tissue removal and still was able to successfully nurse TWO babies. I watched a documentary about a woman who adopted a baby and was able to lactate enough to feed it. I read a book about a woman who couldn't make enough milk for her first baby, but plenty for her second. Some friends and family were unable to get pregnant naturally, and yet their bodies produced the milk they needed for their child's survival without problem. This all devastated me. My broken body got pregnant naturally but couldn't keep the baby alive after. What the fuck. This illogic. This was a jealousy unlike any other because it involved my child. My flesh and blood, my future.

Of course many mothers had so much (unsolicited) advice for me. I was told things like, "Are you drinking enough water? When I was nursing, I just ate more food and then I made more milk. All you need to do is trust your body and the milk will come. Just try a little harder. It will come in. Have you taken fenugreek? Oatmeal? What about offering the breast more often. If you offer formula, the baby will eat less from you. Maybe you need to take a bath and relax. If you relax you will make more milk." Yeah. If I would have fucking taken a bath, everything would have worked out. These unintended insensitivities only intensified my tenacity.

I also had many moms telling me to simply give up. "Formula is fine. You had formula. I had formula. We all turned out ok." My postpartum brain wanted to ask them why they believed they had any right to try and dissuade me from my goals. I responded to these people with blank stares. I thought to myself, "Yeah, I was formula fed and I'm a hot broken mess, and don't even get me started on you." I know these moms were trying to help but their pro-formula agendas just made me cry. I knew I could quit. I knew most people did. But "good enough" just wasn't ok with me. Truly, I didn't give a shit how other people fed their babies. I knew what I wanted to do and that I couldn't do it was the problem.

For months, I merely existed. One day, I had reached a level of exhaustion that required my husband to stay home; I remember sitting cross-legged on my red footstool, unable to think in a complete sentence. I knew that I needed to care for my baby, but I couldn't think of how to do so. I looked at my hands, but was unable to formulate what they were doing. And worse, I was having hallucinations of dropping my new infant or passing out while holding him, crushing him to death. I was losing my grip on reality. I truly couldn't tell what was real. I was scared and so was my husband. He stayed home with me, holding our screaming son while I sat broken, blankly staring into nothingness while being sucked dry.

The pump whirred constantly, the mechanical voice repeating "failure, failure, failure," synchronous with the weak spray of milk dripping leisurely into the Medela bottles almost permanently attached to me; I was part breast pump. My boobs were always out and being sucked into translucent plastic tubes, stretched and vacuumed in the most unnatural way, asexual vestiges of disappointment. Sucked by mechanics instead of my baby, who was growing and changing and beautiful, but only to everyone else.

I couldn't take the Prozac because of the aforementioned liver disease, for fear it would pickle me further. And if I did take it, nursing would be over. No way. So, I saw my shrink who assured me everything would be ok, did some non-traditional treatments, offered some vitamins, but then wondered out loud if there were any other antidepressants that I could take. Girl needed some drugs.

I continued on this path for months. My liver continued to deteriorate. I was put on prednisone, a potent steroid that was somewhat breastfeeding-safe. Wait four hours to nurse or pump after taking a dose. Hope for the best. Pray the drugs don't affect this baby. Try not to die. Try to see through the fog.

Finally, my doctor told me I had one week to wean and then I needed to get back on other not-compatible-with-breastfeeding drugs to save my liver (and my life). I knew the day was coming, I just didn't want to admit it. I considered ignoring his advice and proceeding as usual. My husband and I talked about this and decided it probably wasn't worth further risking my health for a couple more months of nursing. I had been feeling pretty horrible due to the side effects of said liver diseases, which suggested that maybe I should follow the doctor's orders.

The thought of quitting brought me to tears. All this work. Ten and a half months, every day, every night, no exceptions. All the hours for this, whatever this was, coming to an end. My baby wouldn't need me anymore. He was only nursing twice a day and I was only pumping enough for one bottle. But it was something. A part of me for him.

My last night nursing, I held him extra close. He nursed and we snuggled for an hour in the dark bedroom, all the memories of the past months spinning, my own personal movie montage. His little face, his chubby hands softing on my side. Warm, soft, baby belly snugged up to mine. The first day, the last day, and the blur of in-between.

It's been months since I stopped nursing and pumping. In that time, my baby turned into a toddler. He transitioned pretty easily from nursing to none, which was a mixed blessing. Only once did he root around, when he was sick, and my heart broke for the comfort I couldn't give him.

My boobs, however, did not transition so easily. They were pieces of shit. They barely made enough milk for a bottle a day and yet they had the nerve to get clogged ducts and force me to pump and dump multiple times after weaning. I stood shirtless in the mirror many times after watching that precious milk circle the drain, scolding those boobs for their worthlessness. They didn't seem to care and continued to cause me grief. I have never given two shits about my boobs, but after they failed two babies, they failed THE ONLY JOB THEY HAD, fuck them. Double fuck them.

Much of the postpartum depression I experienced was substantially worsened by the semantics of motherhood. The "Breast is Best" doctrine was on repeat in my mind, beaten into me by the "motherhood media," the Teat Nazis (as Tina Fey names them), and the crunchy lactivits who gloated about how wonderful, easy, and absolutely essential nursing was. That I couldn't do this the way I wanted, the RIGHT WAY, destroyed me. I couldn't do the best. And in motherhood in America, if it's not best, it's nothing.

In one of our sessions in coming to terms with this, my shrink told me there were studies that showed "good enough" parenting was actually better than "best" parenting. I have to believe this because I don't have a choice. I also want to believe this because I think it holds merit. We do the best we can. And sometimes the best is just good enough. Sometimes it's organic salad for dinner. And sometimes it's French fries over the sink.

. . .

We're on the floor in the living room, my toddler is "reading" and my daughter is next to him, helping. Their backs are to us and they are chatting away, a forever bond and a language their own. We wish we had the camera to mark this moment, but it can't be marked anyway. None of this can. He has dried egg on his sleeve and his head stinks. Something is crusted near his ear. We can't remember when she last had a shower and the ringworm on her head is smeared with prescription. The house is trashed, with Legos and blocks and books scattered anywhere we might step, likely full of microscopic urine and feces. We slopped together something for dinner, a cacophony from the fridge, and ate off of their plates when they weren't looking. The roof leaks a little in three places, the driveway is crumbling, and grubs have taken over the backyard. But we have these two people, people I grew with my broken body, whom I fed with my broken boobs, and whom we are now guiding through this broken house and this broken world.

My daughter runs to me to define a word, and my son follows, laughing. They plop in my lap, sloppy and with abandon, shoving each other for more of me, joyfully aggressive. She snuggles him and kisses his head, he gives a toothy grin and chews on a toy, both completely in the moment. They sit for less than a minute. But they are there long enough to remind me that they want me, they need me, they love me, I'm good enough. And when they hop up and race away, I watch them from behind, holding hands and smiling into the future, its brokenness part of their excitement.

Not Best for Me

By Kerry Gersonde

October 9, 2018

Today is our oldest child's twelfth birthday and I surprise my-self with tears as I read through my journal from those first two months of her life. We have since had three more children, yet the memories of Juna's birth and subsequent weeks are surprisingly vivid.

On the day she was born, I had a strange sensation that I had known her my entire life, in a way I never felt with the others (although, of course, my love for all of them is equal). Reading through these lengthy journal entries, often with mundane descriptions of all the meals I ate and step-by-step details of my day, I am taken back to the raw emo-tions of those first few weeks parenting a newborn. Today, I mourn Juna's inevitable loss of childhood innocence *and* celebrate her fervent march towards adolescence and even-tual womanhood. My tears also mourn the loss of my own young adulthood and reflect on my heartbreaking naivety as a new mother.

Supported by my husband, mother, medical helpers, and a few friends, I struggled to breastfeed Juna, intent on succeeding because I had learned that "Breast is Best." Although five weeks might seem like a short time, it seemed to last forever, imprinting itself in my memory. In retrospect, I wish I had given up on breastfeeding much sooner. I poured so much energy into figuring out how to make this work, how to make sure my baby was getting enough nutrition while keeping my own body intact, that I was making myself sick. I was sure not to make the same mistake with our next newborns, choosing kindness towards myself, even if that meant supplementing with formula from the beginning.

.   .   .

October 9, 2006

Woke up at 3:00am. My water broke! We're about to go to the hospital. Contractions have started—so far they feel like a stomach ache. We're excited and I'm a little nervous.

The epidural helped the pain of contractions immensely but was a painful procedure because the anesthesiologist accidentally injected it into a vein on the first try, so he had to redo it. Dr. Peterson came in and stayed through the whole pushing phase. Aaron and our doula, Robin, held my legs and Aaron counted through contractions while I pushed. It was painful and difficult. I was nauseated and vomited twice, which helped me push her out. She was born at 12:53pm and Aaron and I were both crying. She had the most beautiful face and head of thick, curly dark hair. They put her on my chest immediately. Aaron and I spent the rest of the day getting to know her and calling friends and family.

October 10, 2006

Morning came quickly. We were overwhelmed with love for Juna. She is the most perfect, precious baby. I spent the day trying to nurse, holding her, looking at her, loving her. I had a severe headache from the epidural so the anesthesiologist came back and gave me a blood patch, taking blood from my arm and injecting it into my back.

October 11, 2006

It was cool and overcast when we left the hospital. Got Juna home and I cried a little—overwhelmed with love and fear. I needed Aaron to clean the house, which he did right away with Mom's help. After Mom left we tried to figure things out and start a routine with Juna. She cried a lot which was hard to watch but normal for her first night home.

October 12, 2006

Had a productive, happy, peaceful day.

October 13, 2006

Went to Juna's first doctor's appointment. He said her weight was down and her sodium was high and he wanted us to start supplementing her feedings with one ounce of formula and come back the next day for a weight check. We went straight to the Birthing Center to see the lactation consultant and were there for two hours. She showed us how to use the pump and nipple shield, syringe, and tube. I got home and started the grueling routine of pumping and feeding through the tube every two hours. Just hoping for some poopy diapers. Did this all afternoon, evening and through the night. Aaron was a great motivator and helper. I broke down crying around 3:00am thinking I couldn't pump anymore. Maybe there's hope but I need to be prepared to accept any outcome. Juna is a beautiful, precious baby. We love her so much it hurts and brings tears to our eyes.

October 14, 2006

Went to Juna's doctor's appointment. We were much more efficient getting ready to go. She weighed eight pounds! She had gained four ounces since Friday. We were so excited we took celebratory photos in the doctor's office.

October 15, 2006

Aaron gave Juna a bath before dinner. I was feeling irritable and exhausted. My nipples are sore and cracked but she's nursing much better.

October 16, 2006

Juna's one week birthday! Aaron got an email from his supervisor asking him to come back to work on Thursday. We were both disappointed. We thought he'd be off the rest of the week. But we accepted it and got on with the rest of our day. Aaron started a fire, Juna is napping, I'm wearing my new robe, life is good.

October 17, 2006

Aaron and I were both exhausted and had a fight in the afternoon. Took a nap and made up from our fight.

October 18, 2006

Called my doctor's office to describe my symptoms—really sore breasts and nipples. The nurse said it sounds like mastitis and called in an antibiotic. Called the lactation consultant and left two messages for the La Leche League women. Feeling frustrated with nursing.

October 19, 2006

My breasts are still very sore and it hurts whenever she latches on. Talked to the doctor and lactation consultant again and they think it's yeast so they called in a prescription for Diflucan. Aaron went to the pharmacy for me twice. We fed Juna breastmilk from the bottle because it was too painful to nurse. She screamed pretty much all night. We got no sleep. About to give up on nursing all together.

October 20, 2006

Called Mom at 5:30am and she came over to help me so I could get some sleep. Juna slept well all day long. We fed her from the bottle while I gave my breasts a rest. Went to my doctor's appointment and he said he supported whatever decision I made. His nurse said if I can get through this it will get better and will be worth it. Feeling so torn.

October 21, 2006

Tried to pump but my right nipple is bleeding. My breasts were hurting again (burning). Doctor called in more Diflucan. I also felt really depressed. Aaron did all the night feedings with pumped breast milk so I could get some sleep.

October 22, 2006

Woke up feeling better—I've read that yeast is more painful at night. Started feeling really tired and sad around 6:00pm. Nursed Juna all night so Aaron could sleep. Beautiful October weather—cool, windy, blue skies, colorful leaves.

October 23, 2006

The beginning of our first full week at home without Aaron. Juna was awake from 9:30am-12:30pm—she would not go to sleep. I have no appetite due to nerves. Took a shower while she screamed in her crib. It was cold and really windy outside—saw some snow flurries. Got dressed and took Juna to the Babes in Arms new mother's support group. I'm glad I went. The other babies are between three and five months so the moms had good advice and made me feel better. Still dealing with a crack on my right nipple. Really painful.

October 24, 2006

Felt like I could never get ahead all day. Juna slept for a while in the Pack 'n Play in the morning and I showered and did a few things around the house. Spent the afternoon dealing with the lactation consultant's recommendations for the yeast and my cracked nipples. Mom came over with all the stuff. I'm supposed to take acidophilus, garlic, echinacea, and grapefruit seed extract. After I nurse, I rinse the breast with water and vinegar then put a homemade ointment on it and let it air dry (equal parts lotrimin antifungal cream, neosporin, and hydrocortisone cream). Mom held Juna while I figured all this stuff out. I'm supposed to eliminate dairy, sugar and bread from my diet. Juna seems to be doing fine—still nursing well despite the cracks and my pain. Aaron came home and seemed exhausted and in a daze from work. We made it through the evening but were both tired. I never even went outside all day. Mom picked up some shells for my bra at the birthing center. They seem complicated to figure out.

October 25, 2006

Tried to take a nap but couldn't fall asleep. Did a load of laundry and pumped a little. Never put on a shirt due to the breast ointment.

October 26, 2006

Went to work for a clinical supervision meeting. Talked to my grad school advisor about my schedule. Still have sore breasts.

October 27, 2006

Sore nipples and my right breast was red and tender. Doctor called in more Diflucan. Aaron came home and we did a gentian violet treatment—turned Juna's mouth purple. Supposed to treat yeast. Obsessed with my breast issues.

October 28, 2006

Juna's first grocery store visit. She slept. Her little mouth is purple from the gentian violet.

November 2, 2006

I felt really tired and kind of depressed. Sore nipples, and ready to give up breastfeeding again. Aaron came home and I cried for a while. He was very comforting and took care of her—she was so fussy. I have night sweats—wake up drenched in sweat.

November 9, 2006

Talked to our doula for advice about switching from breastfeeding to formula and about how to get Juna to sleep.

November 11, 2006

Aaron and I had a fight in the middle of the night, tired and frustrated with Juna crying at 2:00am. We made up before I left to run errands and I apologized for yelling at him. I decided to quit breastfeeding altogether. Relieved to have finally made the decision. In bed by 10:00pm with cabbage leaves in my bra to dry up the milk. Juna woke up at 3:00am and Aaron fed her while I pumped—my breasts were engorged. Still having night sweats.

November 12, 2006

Aaron gave Juna a bath and she projectile vomited. We're completely on formula now. I pumped a little for relief and wore cabbage leaves in my bra. Good day!

.　　.　　.

October 9, 2018

What I would give to have just one of these weeks—or even one day—back with Juna as a newborn. I focused so much on breastfeeding her that I lost precious and fleeting time enjoying her. This was a hard lesson to learn. Parents of older children are often quick to tell us that this time in our lives will fly by. Our children will be graduating from high school, finishing college, getting married, and having babies of their own before we even know what happened. Yet during those long, arduous days of parenting four young children, time seems to creep, leaving me weary and wondering when the fast train will arrive to alleviate the misery.

Of course, it's not all bad—there are plenty of priceless moments and smooth phases that sweeten our lives as parents. During those times especially, I try to remind myself to slow down, be present, and enjoy this. Don't wish this time away because, remember? Remember how much you wish you could have those early days back? How strong the nostalgia pulls you? No doubt I'll be helping any one of them pack the car for college or choose a wedding dress and will pine for one last frustrating, boring, agonizingly slow week of midnight feedings, homework-helping, loud sleepovers, and surprise snow days with these four imaginative, loving, and heartbreakingly beautiful people.

Limbo

By Melissa Kruse

Should. The weighty word that consumes your mind and heart and constantly tells you you're doing the wrong thing. You've made the wrong choice. You should have done something differently. That's Mommy Guilt. I'm waist deep now, with three kids in six years.

When I had my first son, the guilt crept in slowly, starting with returning to work after my twelve week maternity leave. First, *Shouldn't mothers stay home with their kids?* Then, *Why wasn't my body producing enough milk?* A good mom should stay home so she could continue to breastfeed. I guess deep down, that's what I've always considered to be the *right way* to be a mom.

After a while, the mommy guilt waned to an ambient noise that I could pretend to ignore. Then came baby number two. Same song and dance this time around, but the guilt was compounded by the existence of an older child. *Shouldn't a good mother give both children equal love, time, and energy? Shouldn't I have enough patience for everyone? Why can't I balance cook-*

ing, cleaning, laundrying, mothering, and working? Why am I so so so tired? Shouldn't I be able to keep up, like other moms? Shouldn't I be happy in this period of life?

Once my daughter turned one, things became manageable again. The thread of insecurity and inferiority was still an undercurrent, but I wasn't picking myself apart on a regular basis anymore. That is, until my oldest began attending preschool. I wasn't there to drop him off or pick him up. I didn't know his teachers, didn't get to attend his field trips, didn't get to chat with the other moms. The mom-guilt gnawed at me.

When baby three arrived, I decided I had enough with the mommy guilt. I was going to resign from my job, and then everything would be better. I pictured days of playing, laughing, crafts, reading, learning experiences at museums and the park, and possibly even homeschooling. I was going to be home all day! I could clean the house, cook, do laundry, and even read some books. This was the answer.

Practice is always different than premise. My time at home really was a blessing. And also, it wasn't. What I experienced was a whole new set of guilt. But this time, the guilt was because

I didn't like staying at home all day. I loved the *idea* of being with my children more, but in reality, it was hard. There was fighting, crying, poopy diapers, vomit in the car, large orange juice containers spilled in the refrigerator. There was exhaustion, boredom, and an extremely messy house. I missed intellectual stimulation. I missed putting on makeup and showering. I missed having a place to go. I missed going to the bathroom by myself. I missed being part a professional endeavor. I missed connecting with adults.

I was supposed to like staying home. So many moms would jump at the chance! I wasn't ungrateful for it all. But rather than making the guilt disappear, being at home just reversed it. *Shouldn't I appreciate being at home more? Shouldn't I seize this opportunity and play with my daughter during the baby's nap? Shouldn't I volunteer in my son's kindergarten class as often as possible? Shouldn't I? Shouldn't I?*

I wanted to start a business, and did, but the guilt found its way in there, too. I was staying home. *Shouldn't I focus on the kids? Wouldn't it be selfish to take time away from them to pursue a hobby? A dream?*

After my youngest turned two, I decided it was time to go back to work. I yearned to leave the house and teach, my passion. While I hoped that this time would be "guiltless," it wasn't. The guilt is the same. As a teacher now, I feel guilty about being back at work and for wanting to stop staying home. It's my daughter's last year before school. My youngest only has two years left. Shouldn't I have powered through? I could have found a job when they were all in school. I'm mad at myself for going back. I'm annoyed that I love my new job. *Shouldn't I feel guilty for all of this?*

Over the last six years, I've learned that mommy guilt is inescapable. It's a place of limbo. We mothers make one decision, and its consequences lead to more feelings of inadequacy. Being a mom is not a job I ever imagined to be so complex. But it is. It's the hardest thing I've ever done.

To this day, I have to battle the feeling of inferiority. This is at the heart of the mom-guilt. The feeling that I'm not good enough. The truth is that I'm not any different from anyone else. This constant state of limbo, of reflection and nostalgia, of uncertainty—it's not unique to me. Whether I'm working or staying home, whether I'm pursuing my dreams or sacrificing them to put my kids' needs first, it's all part of motherhood. I think what I've learned most is that I'm not alone. *Should?* It's real, and it's stressful, but it doesn't make us bad moms. It means we care. And, we *should.*

A Lesson in Loss: What My Mother Taught Me

By Jill Dawson

"Gosh, I hope that baby gets cuter!" This is what I heard from my mother when my daughter, Delaney, was an infant. Most would be offended by a grandmother insinuating that her infant grand-daughter wasn't cute. But for those who knew Nancy, this statement was a prime example of her glowing (sarcasm) personality.

I come from a line of overbearing, opinionated, stubborn, lovable women. My mother and her mother were women of little tact who never hesitated to tell anyone their opinions. This unsolicited advice only intensified when I, myself, became a mother. Of course, many times I might have needed such bold truth because as mothers, we need all the support we can get. But my mother had an unusual way of dispensing said advice.

My mom was not someone who held back what she was think-ing or feeling; she'd say exactly what was on her mind no matter how blunt. She was honest to a fault and lacked any desire to sugarcoat anything. When I would tell people who didn't know my mother about some of her more honest (usually offensive) statements, said people would look at me, mouth often agape.

"She's very polarizing..." This is how I'd always begin. "People either love her or they don't, but the people who love her, really love her. She's a bit blunt...okay not a bit but a lot blunt and she is not very emotional." To which I would usually get the response, "Oh, wow! Nothing like you." And that couldn't be more true.

Though my mom had a rough, tough "bad reputation to protect" exterior, the many who loved her did so because they knew how great she truly was, hard-hearted facade aside.

My mom was extremely creative. Whether she convinced my dad to sit in the snow in shorts and sandals in the dead of winter with a beer in hand to get the perfect Christmas picture, or to appear dressed only in a towel for another shoot, her Christmas cards were definitely memorable. My Christmas cards aren't nearly as famous, or infamous, as her cards, but her creativity sparked a desire in me to be creative, not only as a mother with my own children, but also in the classroom as a teacher. She also made the holiday season fun for us when we were younger by putting little presents in our stockings for the entire month of December. Each gift was tied to a ribbon with a number. Every morning we pulled the number of the gift that corresponded to which day of December it was. It was like our own little advent calendar, except in this "calendar" we received noisy gifts such as whistles and pieces of candy that she allowed us to eat before school.

My mother was fun and even a little mischievous. During my childhood, Christmas mornings spent at my grandparents' house were filled with excitement for the kids and dread for the adults as there was always a huge mess to clean up. My trickster mom (with the help from my dad) would get all of the nieces and nephews presents that were both amusing and messy, to purposefully add to the chaos. One Christmas, there were boxes filled with shredded paper that contained cans of silly string. When the silly string was found at the bottom of the boxes, there was no holding us kids back from spraying my grandparents' front room (from floor to ceiling) with silly string! This was fun until the Christmas tree lights were covered...and silly string is flammable. There was a mad rush to clean it up so my grandparents' house didn't end up in flames. While the adults were in a frenzy to clean up the mess, my mother just laughed, knowing she would do something equally as messy next year. The more the other adults complained about her shenanigans, the more outlandish the prank would be the next year. Nancy's philosophy of practical joking was, "Spare no expense of money or time!"

In addition to her shenanigans, my mother was giving and selfless. These two traits she tried to hide from everyone and I always told her she was trying to protect her bad reputation by never speaking about her generous side. She showed this generous side in countless ways. In college, I would receive care packages, but sometimes my roommate and dorm floor mates would receive them, too.

Her generous side didn't stop after I graduated college. When I started my current teaching position, I spent a couple of years teaching students who were considered "at risk." She never failed to donate snacks and supplies for me to take to these kids. She never sought acknowledgment for these deeds, and most people had no idea she was supplying my entire classes with what they lacked. She only wanted to make sure no one went without necessities.

Probably her most selfless, giving act of all was that my mother loved and took care of a young man as if he were her biological child. She treated this young man, whom I call my brother, as if he were her own, and then later loved his wife and children in the same vein.

In my lifetime, my mother probably hugged me no more than ten times, and said the words, "I love you," even fewer. But she was a good mother. She taught me to be kind and to accept everyone. The best way to teach someone a skill is to demonstrate it, and she did that with unending consistency. Kindness and acceptance was demonstrated to me and to my own children, if unconventionally. She took my kids on countless adventures, gave them her undivided attention, and never once missed any of their sports events, concerts, or plays. My children were so close to their grandmother that they each had their own relationship with her and they had their own language. They had secrets with her that I will never know and I love that.

When my children were in her care they were given 100 percent of her attention. I would get jealous at times when my kids seemed to love her more than me, but I remember something she told me that made me feel a bit better. She told me that when the kids were at her house, she had the luxury of giving them all of her attention because when they went home, that's when she could do all of her household chores. When the grandkids where at her house, the laundry and cleaning could wait. As full-time mothers who also run households, we don't get that luxury. She told me that as their mom, I had the struggle of balancing parenting and maintaining a home and career. And I always appreciated that my mom tried to ease my mind when I felt as if my kids loved her more (which they still probably did).

With all of her seeming contradictory traits, my mother was the strongest woman I will ever know. While my mom suffered over the last year from cancer, she also battled a degenerative neck disorder that was debilitating. I never once heard her complain about either of these ailments. She could have wallowed in self-pity, but she never did. She just tried to live her life as normally as possible. I also think she didn't want others to know how sick she was because she wouldn't have wanted others' pity. She never talked about what her treatments were like and she never wanted anyone to accompany her to those treatments. Last summer, when I finally came to the realization that her cancer was getting worse, I started to go with her to her treatments. She hated every second of this. I told her that I didn't care and that I was going with her whether she liked it or not because I know she would have done that for me. She knew that was true, but that fact did not make her any more accepting of me there. This woman had opinions.

My mother and I couldn't have been more dissimilar. I came out of the womb a natural-born rule-follower; she thrived on rebellion. She had little tact; I am mortified to ever offend anyone or make someone feel upset. One would think these differences would have made for more distance in our relationship, but somehow she became my best friend. I told her everything. I went to her for advice, and even though I didn't always like or agree with the advice she gave to me, I took it to heart. She somehow always knew the best advice to give to me. This wasn't always appreciated while I was growing up; however, as soon as I became an adult, I knew she was right.

My mother died when I was forty-three years old. Though she had been ill, this death was sudden and I don't think I have or ever truly will come to terms with the void she's left in our lives. By losing her, we lost a constant source of support, unconditional love, tough love, and friendship.

Today, almost on a daily basis, I find myself wanting to pick up the phone to call her. Whether to vent, share a story about what the kids are doing, or to ask for her signature tactless advice, I miss our conversations. It's tough going through life without your mom, even as a woman in her forties. I don't know why but thinking about her in the quiet moments I have to myself is tough, but talking about her to people isn't. Keeping her memory alive for my children is vitally important to me. She was an enormous part of their lives, and that will never change. A song will come on that she liked, or something funny will happen and I find myself saying to my kids, "That was Grandma's favorite song." or "What do you think Grandma would say about that?" Because she had a lot to say, and just because she is gone, her voice is not.

Her tactless voice, her mischievous ways, and her huge heart for people made me the mother I am today. Even though my mother and I couldn't have been more dissimilar in our personalities, she taught me how to be empathetic, giving, creative, and strong. As mothers, we need all the love and support we can get. We all know that motherhood does not come with an instruction manual.

For nine months, women grow other humans inside of their bodies, which is a tough job. But then those tiny humans make their appearance in the world and we are expected to have this innate understanding of what we're supposed to do with them. That's when, if we're lucky enough, our own mothers step in to help. My mother may have given me unsolicited advice on many occasions, but I learned many lessons from her. Many of these lessons help me to be a better mother. And just to be clear, my mom eventually did believe and openly admit that when my daughter Delaney got older, she did get a whole lot cuter.

Dear Mom

By Jackie Armich

Dear Mom,

How did you do it? I mean, really. You were just sixteen years old when you had Christie. Sixteen years old with a newborn and a shitty husband and poor, poor, poor. And then a mere eighteen months later, I was born. You had just graduated high school. We've never really talked about how you felt becoming a mother that young, but if we ever did, I would tell you that I truly cannot imagine being in your situation. I'm amazed and impressed with your determination. Nearly forty years later, there are still countless girls who end up having to drop out of high school because they become mothers, and you didn't. You faced all challenges with love and pure grit. For us.

My first memories are from when we lived with grandma and grandpa. I guess I would've been three or four. You would've been about twenty years old. We lived in the upstairs, you on one side, and Christie and me on the other. You worked at Thrift-T Mart, and I remember going in with you when you worked in the deli. You sat me on a counter in the back and I watched you do your work. You were probably annoyed that you had to bring me in, but I remember thinking it was so fun to see you at work. And looking back, I'm sure you had no choice.

When I was a little older and we moved to the apartment on Ivy Lane, I have fond memories of being down the street from Aunt Maureen. I was in kindergarten, and we would take the bus to her house after school. She would watch us until you got off of work, and I remember Stephanie babysitting us sometimes, too. You always made sure we were taken care of while you worked your ass off to provide for us. In the summer, Christie and I would play outside while you laid out on a lawn chair between the two brick apartment buildings. We had no idea how much you struggled and worked for us to have moments like those.

I always remember having food to eat, a clean place to live, and decent clothes to wear. Looking back, it's apparent to me that we were very poor. I never felt poor as a child, though. You somehow made us believe we could have anything we needed. You also were THERE for us, wanting to spend time and do fun things with us. I remember trips with you to the state park or to the zoo or to your best friend's house. You did all of this with no money, with no support, and with two small kids always tugging at your sides.

And now I am about to turn forty. I have two kids of my own and I feel so lucky. I have a college education (a master's degree even), a decent and secure job, an awesome, supportive husband, a house, a car, and the ability to provide anything needed for my family. You tell me often that you're proud of me, that I'm a good mom, and that I have a great husband. And I thank my lucky stars all the time that I am not in a different situation. While I don't know how this hand of cards was dealt to me, I think it has much to do with you.

I watched you be the badass mother that you are my entire life, and in your modeling, I am now that badass mother. I am able to give my girls basically anything they could want. I don't, though. I try to hold back. I don't want my children to be "spoiled" into thinking life will give them anything they desire. I want them to understand the importance of working hard to get what they want, like I was able to learn from you. This lesson was one of the most important that you taught us. And I'm sure it was a hard lesson to teach because you didn't have a choice other than to work and mother as hard as you could.

And for that, I am so grateful. Thank you for all that you did for us as kids and for all you do for me now. I hope you enjoyed watching us grow up as much as I'm now loving watching my own daughters. Everything I'm good at now is directly related to you. Thank you.

Love You to the Moon and Back,

Jackie

Acknowledgments

Thank you to the women who were brave enough to contribute their very personal and sometimes painful stories to this collective. I am honored to be so trusted. Thank you to my parents for all the support necessary to raise children of my own, and to be the independent and stubborn woman that I am. Thank you to Carrie Gingerich for proofreading this book while parenting, moving, and working full-time during a pandemic—I owe you! Thank you to Sam for patiently laying this book out and designing the cover with me aggressively demanding changes over your shoulder. And lastly, thank you to my children for making me a mother and for giving me the reason to create this book.

Made in the USA
Middletown, DE
23 November 2020

24949462R00166